VAQUEROS

VAQUEROS

AMERICA'S FIRST COWMEN

MARTIN W. SANDLER

HENRY HOLT AND COMPANY

NEW YORK

Henry Holt and Company, LLC
Publishers since 1866
115 West 18th Street
New York, New York 10011

Henry Holt is a registered trademark of Henry Holt and Company, LLC

Published in Canada by Fitzhenry & Whiteside Ltd., 195 Allstate Parkway,
Markham, Ontario L3R 4T8.

Library of Congress Cataloging-in-Publication Data
Sandler, Martin W.
Vaqueros: America's first cowmen / Martin W. Sandler.
p.   cm.
Includes bibliographical references and index.
1. Mexican American cowboys—History—Juvenile literature.   I. Title.
E184.M5 S256   2000   973'.046872—dc21   00-24285

ISBN 0-8050-6019-7
First Edition—2001
Printed in the United States of America on acid-free paper.∞
1 3 5 7 9 10 8 6 4 2

Photos courtesy of the Library of Congress except the following: Pages
6–7, 17, 46, 65 courtesy of the Gilcrease Museum, Tulsa ("Wild
Horses" by James Walker, 0126.1538; "Hacendado y Su Mayordomo"
by T. Lanhert, 1549.49; "Vaqueros in a Horse Corral" by James Walker,
0126.1480; "Vaqueros Lassoing a Bear" by James Walker); page 11
from the US Department of Transportation; pages 12, 13, 15, 44, 101
courtesy of the University of Texas Institute of Texan Cultures (No. 75-
1286; No. 88-371; No. 72-261; No. 75-337; No. 82-423); pages 14,
32, 34, 73 courtesy of the Texas Department of Transportation; page 16
courtesy of the California State Library; photo 21 courtesy of the
National Archives; page 28 courtesy of the California Historical Soci-
ety; pages 42, 59 from the author's collection; page 56 courtesy of the
R. W. Norton Gallery; page 74 courtesy of the San Francisco Union
League Club; page 86 courtesy of the National Cowboy Hall of Fame,
Oklahoma City; page 91 copyright © Underwood & Underwood/
CORBIS; pages 95, 96, 97, 98, 103 courtesy of the American Folklife
Center.

CONTENTS

Introduction   *vii*

Chapter One
    HORSES, CATTLE, AND A SPECIAL BREED OF MEN   3

Chapter Two
    THE VAQUEROS INVENT THE COWBOY   10

Chapter Three
    THE VAQUERO AS A PERSON   24

Chapter Four
    THE VAQUEROS' SPECIAL SKILLS   39

Chapter Five
    VAQUEROS AT WORK: A PICTURE ESSAY   52

Chapter Six
    TALES OF THE VAQUEROS   61

Chapter Seven
    THE VAQUERO BECOMES INVISIBLE   76

Chapter Eight
    COWMEN TODAY   93

Sources   *105*

Glossary   *109*

Further Reading   *111*

Index   *113*

INTRODUCTION

The story you are going to read is about courageous and skillful men who have never received the credit due them for all they contributed to the building of America. They were called vaqueros, and long before anyone ever imagined that there would someday be American cowboys, they rode the ranges of Mexico and large parts of what would become the United States.

I first encountered the vaqueros while doing research for a book on the cowboys. Like most people, I had never questioned how these men who came to be legendary figures got their start. Naively, I imagined that they developed all that went into being a cowboy as they went along.

I was dead wrong. For what I was amazed to discover was that some three hundred years before the first American cowboy roped his first steer or mounted his first bucking bronco, thousands of vaqueros were raising tens of thousands of cattle and were inventing all the tools and techniques that would one day turn almost half of the United States into a cattle empire.

What fascinated me most, however, were the vaqueros themselves. As I delved deeper into the subject I learned that they routinely performed feats of riding and roping that have never been surpassed. I discovered that the courage they continually displayed was every bit as great as that possessed by the most celebrated heroes in the fiction that we read.

All of this left me with giant questions. If, in fact, these Hispanic cowmen had invented the art of being a cowboy by passing on all they knew to the American cowpunchers, why is there so little known about them? If they were among the most skilled and daring of all individuals, why is there so little about them for us to read?

Searching deeper, I found the disturbing answer. Just as African-Americans, Asians, and other minority groups would suffer the consequences of racial and ethnic prejudice, the vaqueros were also the victims of discrimination. While the American cowboy would become our most celebrated hero, the story of the vaqueros would often be purposely ignored or distorted.

For me, writing this book has been a genuine adventure. I have been happily forced into searching for whatever material about the vaqueros I could find. In telling their story I have discovered important pieces of information about them scattered through the writings of such articulate old-time observers of the West as Frederic Remington and J. Frank Dobie.

By poring through the writings of western correspondents for such early publications as *Harper's Weekly* and

Frank Leslie's Illustrated Newspaper I have gained knowledge of the vaqueros' way of life. I have also benefited from the insights into the vaqueros' character provided by the work of such modern historians and authors as Félix D. Almaráz, Jr., Timothy M. Matovina, David Montejano, Américo Paredes, and Richard D. Slatta.

My search for information about the deeds of individual vaqueros has been aided by staff members of such institutions as the Institute of Texan Cultures, the Center for Mexican American Studies, and the American Folklife Center at the Library of Congress. Finally, I owe a great debt to Marc Aronson of Henry Holt and Company. If, in this book, I have achieved what I set out to do it is because of his constant urging to "make the vaqueros come alive." Given who they were, what they contributed, and how they have been neglected, the vaqueros' fascinating and important story needs to be told.

MARTIN W. SANDLER
COTUIT, MASSACHUSETTS

CHAPTER ONE

HORSES, CATTLE, AND A SPECIAL BREED OF MEN

Long before the American cowboys made their appearance, vaqueros rode the ranges and cattle trails of Mexico and vast areas of what became part of the United States. The word vaquero comes from the Spanish *vaca,* or cow. Vaqueros were cowmen, and they may have been the greatest horsemen the world has ever known. Their skill with a rope has never been surpassed. Almost everything an American cowboy did, the clothing he wore, the equipment he used, the special words he spoke, even the values he held dear came directly from the vaqueros. Here is their story.

Some 120 years ago, Frederic Remington, the great artist of the West, visited a cattle ranch in Mexico. While there he witnessed a scene he would never forget. "In the morning," he wrote, "we could see from the ranch-house a great semicircle of gray on the yellow plains. It was the thousands of cattle coming to the *rodeo* (roundup). In an hour more we

A vaquero on horseback with rope, as he appeared in Harper's Weekly *in 1885.*

"On the prairies," wrote J. Frank Dobie, "[longhorns] . . . could run like antelopes; in the thickets of thorn and tangle they could break their way with the agility of panthers." But what fascinated observers most about the animals was the size of their horns. Legend had it that the longhorns would be safe from falling into crevices because their horns would hang over the sides.

could plainly see the cattle, and behind them the vaqueros dashing about waving their *serapes* (capes). Gradually they converged on the *rodeo* ground, and, enveloped in a great cloud of dust and with hollow bellowings, like the low pedals of a great organ, they began to mill, or turn about a common center. Here one sees the matchless horsemanship of the [vaqueros]. Their [horses], trained to the business, respond to the slightest pressure."

The cattle that Remington observed were amazing creatures. They were descendants of animals that had been

At one time, hundreds of thousands of mustangs roamed wild both in Mexico and on land that would one day become a large part of the United States. The

tended for more than a thousand years on the Spanish plains and the grasslands of northern Africa. Their horns often measured up to five feet from tip to tip, which won them the name of longhorns.

vaqueros' roping and riding skills allowed them to capture whatever wild horses they needed for their work.

Longhorns came in various colors—black, red, yellow, white, and spotted. At maturity, they weighed about 1,600 pounds. J. Frank Dobie, one of the most talented of all writers of the cattle country, understood the special value of the longhorn: "With their steel hoofs, their long legs, their stag-like muscles, their thick skins, their powerful horns, [long-horns] could walk the roughest ground, cross the wildest deserts, climb the highest mountains, swim the wildest rivers, fight off the fiercest bands of wolves, endure hunger, cold, thirst and punishment as few beasts of the earth have ever shown themselves capable of enduring."

The longhorn was the perfect animal for the cattle raising that grew up first in Mexico and then in the United States. The longhorns' ability to travel enormous distances without sleep or drink enabled them to thrive on the vast North American range. They were well suited to lengthy cattle drives stretching thousands of miles—as long as savvy cow-men kept them in line.

The horses that Remington described were as amazing as the longhorns. They, too, could not have been better bred for the vital role they played in the cow country. They had originally been brought into Spain from northern Africa by African Muslims known as Moors. The Spanish called these horses *mesteños,* but in America they became known as mustangs. Mustangs stood about five feet high. They could run extremely fast and had great endurance. Like the long-horns, they adapted quickly to North America.

Mustangs had an extraordinary kind of intelligence that can best be described as "cow sense." They had an instinc-tive ability to control even the most cantankerous long-horns. A mustang could anticipate a longhorn's every move, separate it from the herd, and lead it in a desired direction, often without any commands from the cowhand who rode him. As one noted historian put it, the mustang was "a natural-born cow horse and without him and his companion longhorn part of America could never have been built." He might well have added another companion— the vaquero.

The men who rode the mustangs, tended the cattle, and invented all the techniques of cattle raising in America were called vaqueros, and they were the world's first cowboys.

CHAPTER TWO

THE VAQUEROS INVENT THE COWBOY

COWS COME TO AMERICA

The vaqueros' story begins with Christopher Columbus. In 1493, the explorer made his second voyage from Spain to the New World and landed on the island of Hispaniola, which today contains both the Dominican Republic and Haiti. Columbus brought with him thirty-five horses and an unknown number of cattle. The horses were the first to set foot in the Americas since the prehistoric horses of the Ice Age became extinct. The cattle were the first ever to appear in the New World.

The animals multiplied rapidly, and over the next three decades many were taken from Hispaniola to Mexico. At this time, Mexico and all the land that would someday be Texas, California, and the American Southwest were under Spanish claim. In these early days Spanish conquistadors were primarily interested in uncovering the riches, mainly gold, that were rumored to exist in the ancient Indian empires of the Americas.

In 1521, the Spanish military leader Hernán Cortés succeeded in conquering the Aztecs in Mexico and set about plundering them of vast amounts of gold, jewels, and other treasures. A year later, Gregorio de Villalobos transported a large herd of cattle from Hispaniola to the region of Mexico that Cortés had conquered. Within a few months, Cortés himself became the New World's first cattleman by establishing a ranch on the land he had taken over from the Aztecs. He called his ranch Cuernavaca, an adaptation of the Spanish words for cow horn.

In the first half of the 1500s, Spanish explorers and adventurers followed in the footsteps of Christopher Columbus by bringing horses and cattle from Spain. The Spanish brought the cattle for the meat and hides they provided. They used the horses to transport themselves and their men.

In 1540, another Spanish seeker of riches, Francisco Vásquez de Coronado, made his contribution to New World cattle raising. Coronado was convinced that the legendary Golden Cities of Cíbola were located in an area north of Mexico. Determined to capture the vast treasures he believed were there, he organized an ambitious expedition of men and supplies. As part of this expedition he took with him five hundred head of cattle.

Coronado never was able to find any cities of gold. But by taking longhorns into what would become the American Southwest, he introduced the first cattle of any kind into what is now the United States. In the process, Coronado and his men became the New World's first trail drivers.

By the middle of the 1600s, enormous herds of the fast-

This scene, drawn some two decades before serious ranching began in the United States, shows vaqueros driving a herd of longhorns through a square in Veracruz, Mexico.

Over the course of almost two hundred years, an unbroken bond developed between the land, the cattle, and the men known as vaqueros.

multiplying cattle and wild horses roamed freely on the Mexican plains while Spanish adventurers continued to bring cattle and horses northward. At the same time, another group of men began to make their presence felt. They were Catholic priests, or *padres,* sent to the Americas to convert the natives to Christianity.

Many of the missions that the padres built were beautiful structures. They often surrounded them with fortresses known as presidios, put there to protect the missions from bandits, raiding bands of Indians, and the adventurers from other European nations challenging Spanish claim to their New World territory.

In the very earliest days of their life on the mission ranches, some vaqueros used long lances to help them move the cattle along.

ON THE MISSIONS

The *padres* worked very hard. They supervised the building of missions, many of them large and well constructed. The missions contained churches as well as many kinds of work spaces. One of the earliest was the mission of Nuestra Señora de los Dolores established in 1687 by Father Eusebio Kino in what is now the Mexican state of Sonora, near Arizona. Beginning in 1769, Father Junípero Serra led a group of Franciscan friars who built a chain of twenty-one missions that stretched along six hundred miles of the California coast.

Building the missions was one thing; earning enough money to keep them operating was another. But the *padres* found a way. Many of them were the sons of noblemen

In this early sketch, vaqueros drive a herd of cattle past a California mission. Cattle on California missions were not raised for their beef but for their hides and for their fat, which produced tallow, the main ingredient used in candles and soap.

back in Spain, and as youngsters they had been trained to handle cattle on their family ranches. They looked around and saw the ever-growing herds of cattle and horses roaming free. Clearly they could make money by establishing ranches on their mission property and selling the products that would come from the animals they raised. But they also knew that in order to make their ranches successful they would need a lot of help. Out of this need came the vaqueros.

For more than a hundred years, Mexican cowhands who took the name vaqueros worked the mission ranches. There

The wealthy Mexican landowners known as charros, on whose ranches tens of thousands of vaqueros worked, carried on the legacy of the gentleman riders of Spain.

they honed their riding and roping skills and invented the American version of the cowman. Then things began to change.

CHARRO LIFE

In 1821, Mexico freed itself from Spain. The leaders of the new Mexican nation were unhappy with the power and wealth that the Church had accumulated through ranching. They began to encourage cattle raising away from the missions by granting huge tracts of land to wealthy Mexican

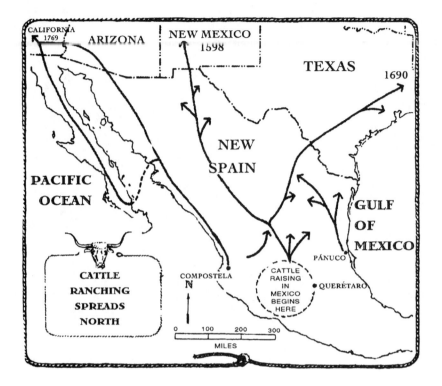

gentlemen known as *charros*. Vaqueros soon went to work on these growing cattle spreads.

Despite these efforts, by 1834 more than 30,000 vaqueros were still tending some 396,000 cattle and 62,000 horses on the mission ranches. Then the Mexican government abruptly took the mission ranches away from the *padres*. The outraged priests responded by ordering the destruction of their herds. The vaqueros on the mission ranches did not have to look far for new employment. They went to work for the *charros,* and it was on their ranches that they perfected their methods of tending the cattle, rounding them up, branding them, and trail-driving them to market.

NORTHBOUND ROUTES OF CATTLE DRIVES FROM TEXAS

TEJAS AND TEXAS

By the 1830s, thousands of vaqueros were at work in Mexico and in Mexican territories. Soon their world would be greatly expanded. In 1836, Texas won its independence from Mexico and became a republic. Nine years later it became part of the United States. Vaqueros who had long worked on ranches in Tejas (the name given to Texas when it belonged to Mexico) were suddenly now on United States soil. In America, vaqueros were central to the largest cattle-raising venture the world has ever known.

In the late 1860s, with the Civil War finally over and Americans in eastern cities clamoring for beef, ranchers in states throughout the American Southwest saw the oppor-

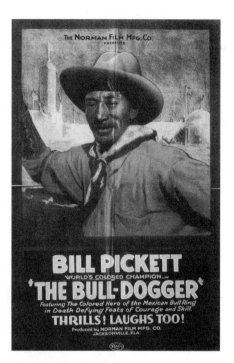

One of the most remarkable of all the African-American cowboys was a man named Bill Pickett, who invented a whole new way of bringing down a steer. After roping the steer, Pickett leaped from his horse, grabbed the animal by the horns, and twisted its neck, turning the steer's face upward. He then bit the steer's lower lip much as a bulldog would do. The action caused the animal to fall over from both pain and shock. Pickett's technique was labeled bulldogging.

tunity to make fortunes raising cattle. In turn, more and more young men were anxious to escape the crowded cities and rushed out west to take up the life of the cowboy. These new white American cowboys learned their trade from the thousands of vaqueros who had been hired by ranch owners well aware of their skills and experience. They were joined also by some five thousand African-Americans who saw in the life of the cowboy the opportunity to experience a greater sense of freedom than they had ever enjoyed. Some

Paniolos:
Vaqueros Across the Sea

The vaqueros were responsible for the birth of the cowman in one of the unlikeliest of places—across the Pacific Ocean in the Hawaiian Islands. It is a fascinating story.

In 1793, a man named George Vancouver brought the first cattle to Hawaii. They were his gift to the Hawaiian king. The grateful monarch placed the cattle under royal protection, forbidding anyone to

Hawaiian vaqueros (paniolos).

slaughter a cow. For the next ten years, the cattle multiplied in great numbers until there were large herds roaming the fertile Hawaiian grasslands. In 1803, another American, Richard Cleveland, brought his own gift to the king. It was a herd of mustangs that had been raised in Spanish California.

In 1832, a new Hawaiian king came to the conclusion that the combination of the growing herds of cattle, the large number of horses, and the presence of huge, open grassland areas provided the opportunity for the establishment of a profitable cattle industry in his nation. He also realized that he needed skilled men to tend the cattle. The king asked vaqueros who had been working ranches in Mexico to come to Hawaii to teach Hawaiians all the techniques of ranching.

The vaqueros who answered the king's call trained the emerging Hawaiian cowboys in all the aspects of cattle raising. The Hawaiians even borrowed the vaqueros' name. They called themselves *paniolos,* a Hawaiian adaptation of the word vaquero. Thanks to the vaqueros, Hispanic cowboy culture was transferred to the Pacific long before the American cowboys appeared on the range, and more than one hundred years before Hawaii became an American state.

of these men, such as Nat Love, became known for their skills and courage in handling cattle. One black cowboy, Jessie Stahl, was regarded by many observers as the best rider of wild horses in the West.

Most of the ranches established in the United States were far larger than the spreads the vaqueros had worked in Mexico. Some, like the King and Kenedy ranches, were as many as sixty miles long and nine miles wide. Operations on these ranches were on a gigantic scale. By the late 1870s, some American roundups involved vaqueros and other cowhands from as many as twenty different ranches and covered an area of more than one hundred square miles. Cattle drives to railroad centers in Kansas required cowhands to trail cattle more than eighteen hundred miles and took from two to three months to complete.

As they worked alongside cowboys, vaqueros passed on to them all that they knew. Some cowboys even called themselves buckaroos, a variation of the word vaquero. The cowboys did make some changes, particularly in the vocabulary of the range. The vaqueros' *chaparajos* (pant coverings) became chaps; *tapaderas* (leather feet protectors) were simply called taps; a cowboy's saddle was held in place by a cinch, rather than the vaqueros' *cincha.*

But the work of the American ranch was essentially the same as that introduced by the vaqueros more than a hundred years earlier. And the American cowboy was who he was because of the men who had ridden the Mexican ranges. One historian of the West put it best, "The American cowboy who rapidly became such a symbol of our culture is basically a revamped vaquero."

CHAPTER THREE

THE VAQUERO AS A PERSON

A CENTURY OF LOYALTY

Who was this man, this vaquero? What was he like? Vaqueros prized loyalty both to their *compañeros* (fellow vaqueros) and to the ranch owners who paid their wages. Faustina Villa, for example, was a vaquero whose loyalty to the owner of the King Ranch on which he worked became the subject of stories told throughout the cattle country. There was the time in the 1870s that the owner urgently needed to get a letter to his lawyer. The problem was that the message had to be carried across the flooded San Gertrudis Creek. Villa, knowing how important it was that the letter be delivered, volunteered to perform the task. He accomplished this by swimming a half mile across the swift-moving water. When he did this, Faustina Villa was one hundred years of age.

Almost all the clothing and equipment the vaqueros introduced to the range served a purpose. To protect his pants and legs from being torn apart as he rode through razor-sharp undergrowth and thicket, a vaquero wore sturdy overalls called chaparajos. *Around his neck he wore a neckerchief called a bandana, which he wound around his ears in cold weather and wrapped around his nose and mouth as protection against the constant dust kicked up by the horses and cattle. Atop his head sat a high-crowned, enormously wide-brimmed hat called a* sombrero, *which guarded him against the rays of the scorching sun.*

The loyalty displayed by vaqueros was so constant that it came to be expected of them. One time Ignacio Alvarado, another King Ranch vaquero, was two days late for his job of leading a herd of cattle on a trail drive. His employer could not understand why the always dependable vaquero was so tardy. Finally, Alvarado's son arrived at the ranch.

"My father says to tell you he cannot come," stated the young man.

"Why?" asked the employer.

"He says he is sorry, but he has to stay home to die."

BULL-TAILING AND MAD COURAGE

The sense of loyalty that marked the vaqueros was matched by their courage. Those who observed them marveled at the way they would ride into the middle of a stampeding herd in order to bring it under control, or would ride for hours without food in the worst types of weather to track down a stray animal. This was always done without complaining. A vaquero took it for granted that these risks were part of his job, that he would do whatever was required of him, and that he would do it well.

Bulls and vaqueros were a match made in heaven, or hell. "They go boldly into the corral with the maddened brutes," reported Frederic Remington, "seeming to pay no heed to the imminent possibilities of a trip to the moon. They toss their ropes and catch the bull's feet, they skillfully avoid his rush, and in a spirit of bravado they touch the horns, pat him on the back, or twist his tail."

Twisting a ferocious bull's tail began on the range, where it served a real purpose. "A huge bull, wild with fright," wrote Remington, "breaks from the herd, with lowered head and whitened eye, and goes charging off indifferent to what or whom he may encounter. . . . A man will pursue a bull at top speed, will reach over and grasp the tail of the animal, bring it to his saddle, throw his right leg over the tail and swing his horse suddenly to the left, which throws the bull rolling over and over. This method has its value . . . when an unsuccessful throw was made with the rope, and the animal was about to enter thick timber; it would be impossible to coil the rope again, and an escape would follow but for the wonderful dexterity of these men." Bull-tailing was so difficult that it was one of the few techniques that the American cowboys did not borrow from the vaqueros. Even the rough-and-ready cowboys regarded it as too dangerous to try.

A MAN'S WORD

Contrary to what many prejudiced Anglo-Americans later wrote about them, most vaqueros were extremely honest and took pride in the fact that their word was their bond. "My work," stated an old-time cowboy, "took me among various Mexican rancheros, and I want to say here that I found them strictly honest. When we found our cattle among theirs, they would tell us frankly that the cattle were not theirs, but at the same time they requested proof of our right to them. This proof was readily given [and the cattle returned]."

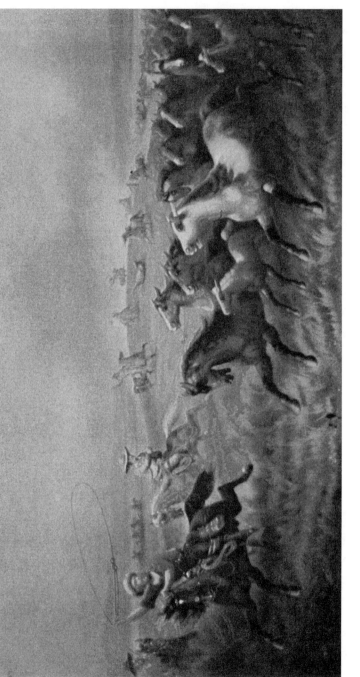

Bringing a herd of wild horses under control was but one of the countless ways in which vaqueros continually demonstrated their courage. The artist titled this picture Californios at the Horse Roundup. Californios was the name often given to the vaqueros who worked the ranges of California.

A dramatic example of the honesty that was part of the Hispanic ranching tradition can be found in the story of two friends who owned ranches on the Mexican–United States border during the last two decades of the 1800s. One of these men, Eusebio García, belonged to a family that had owned its Mexican ranch for generations. García's American neighbor, Tom Coleman, was part owner of the Callaghan Ranch.

At the time, many ranch owners had begun erecting oil wells on their property in hope of striking it rich. One day, while riding the range together, the two friends struck a deal. They agreed that if by chance oil was found on García's land or if one of Coleman's wells brought in oil, each would give

Vaquero pride as well as courage led them to believe that they could master any horse, no matter how wild. The artist who created this fanciful drawing captured the humor that often accompanied the vaqueros' determination to tame any beast.

What the Vaqueros Ate

Both on Mexican and United States ranches, meal-time was one of the few opportunities a vaquero had to relax. This was especially true if he was fortunate enough to be off the range and could partake of a meal at the ranch. Most of the time, however, he was on the range where meals on the open ground at the chuck wagon or taken alone on the far reaches of the range were far from luxurious.

Vaqueros loved to eat meat, but it was only available if they were lucky enough to capture wild game such as deer or elk. Although they were surrounded by cattle, they would never think of slaughtering one of the animals. The vaqueros' whole reason for being was to make sure the cattle stayed healthy and were in the best condition possible so they could be sold at the highest price.

On the range and on cattle drives vaqueros ate a monotonous diet of bread, especially *tortillas*, beans, bacon, and endless quantities of coffee. On the American range, vaqueros and cowboys were

> served a round bread called *pan de campo* (camp bread), which the cook baked in a portable oven.

the other a lease on forty acres of the land where the "black gold" was found. The deal was struck solely on the basis of a handshake and was never put in writing.

Some time later, Tom Coleman suffered severe financial losses. At about the same time, a rich oil field was discovered on Eusebio García's land. Shortly afterward, a mutual friend of the two men was invited by Coleman to view oil wells on García's property. He was surprised to find a happy Coleman, who gave no indication of having come upon hard times.

When they reached the oil wells in a section of García's ranch, Coleman proudly announced that these particular wells belonged to him and the oil from the wells had dramatically reversed his fortunes. Asked to explain, he stated simply that he owed it all to the word of his Mexican friend.

SHOWERS OF GOLD

Although most vaqueros took up the life of the range while very young and had little schooling, many developed keen insights based on day-to-day experiences and observations rather than on knowledge gained from books. To survive, vaqueros had to learn to read the natural world as if it were a book. No matter what region of the cattle country they

Typical of the scores of varieties of vegetation that grew in the cattle country was the plant known as claret cup. The vaqueros knew that although the plant's blossoms were strikingly beautiful its thorns were particularly vicious and had to be carefully avoided.

worked in, most vaqueros could identify each type of bush or plant that grew on the open range and could tell which vegetation was harmful to themselves and their horses and cattle.

The vaqueros knew that hidden throughout the beautiful foliage of plants like the *coma,* the *brasil,* and the *clepino* were multitudes of daggerlike thorns that could tear the flesh of any human or animal that wandered or raced through them. They were particularly aware of the retama with its stunning array of yellow flowers, which vaqueros called *illuvia de oro* (shower of gold). Despite its beauty, it was among the most lethal of all plants, containing thorns that could penetrate deeper than almost any other growth. And whether they were young or older cowhands, vaqueros understood that any thicket that contained bushes known as cat's claw, plants with tentaclelike branches that wrapped themselves around a person or animal and seemed never to let go, were to be avoided at any cost.

Vaqueros also had to learn which plants were useful. They knew, for example, that the one true sign that spring was finally arriving was the sight of the first buds of the fragrant *agrito*, always the first plant to bloom on the range. They were aware that, despite its vicious thorns, the *coma* contained large clusters of delicious blueberries hidden within its leaves. They picked through thickets of *granjeno* bushes and harvested their succulent yellow berries. When they were ill, they took the leaves of the *amargosa* plant and ground it into a healing tea. And when a vaquero was bitten by a rattlesnake, his companions searched frantically for the leaves of a plant called Spanish dagger that gave off a natural serum which was an effective antidote to the deadly bite. Most important, all vaqueros knew that the *huajilla* plant, which overspread the range, was the most nourishing of all vegetation in North America for their cattle and horses to graze on.

J. Frank Dobie put it best. The vaquero, he wrote, "is familiar with the habits of every creature of his soil. For him every hill and hollow has a personality and a name. . . . He knows that name and virtue of every brush and herb. He is a child of nature; he is truly *un hombre del campo* (a man of the land)."

The moon shining over the cattle region often provided a spectacular sight. But it was their knowledge of the different phases of the moon that was most important to the vaqueros. It helped them predict weather conditions and enabled them to know when the land they traveled upon would be brightest or darkest at night.

TELLING TIME BY THE STARS

The vaqueros needed to know as much about the sky as the earth around them. They carried no watches, but used the stars as their timepieces. They were aware, for example, that the Big Dipper swung completely around the North Star every twenty-four hours. By noting the position of the "pointers" of the Dipper in relation to the star they could tell what time it was at night with almost uncanny accuracy. This ability was particularly important in determining when it was time to change the night guard of the horses and cattle.

Their knowledge of the location of other stars was very useful to them as well. The appearance of the Morning Star was the signal for the cook to begin making breakfast and for the vaqueros in charge of the horses to start getting the animals ready for the day's work.

Along with using the heavens to tell time, vaqueros also knew how to calculate the various phases of the moon. Their method, called *la Epcata*, had been handed down to them by early Mexican ranchers and was based on carefully observing the position of the sun in relation to that of the moon.

The moon told the vaqueros many things. By understanding when there would be little moonlight, they could plan when it was necessary to be particularly alert against horse thieves who operated in the dark. By knowing when the moon would be full and would give off maximum light, they could plan when would be the best time, if necessary, to march their herds through difficult mountain passes at night.

COW SENSE

Through careful observation, the vaqueros learned everything about the animals they tended, even how the animals thought. They understood, for example, that cattle usually divide themselves off into small groups with an older cow or bull as each group's leader. They knew that on the range these groups stayed off by themselves and sought water in the same watering tank each day. This enabled the vaqueros, when rounding up the herds on the vast range, to know

Other Latin American Cowmen

The vaqueros were not the only men who transferred the rich Spanish tradition of horsemanship and ranching to the New World. After sixteenth-century conquistadors brought over horses and cattle from Spain, cattle raising developed in several Latin American nations.

In Argentina, cowmen known as *gauchos* rode the region known as the Pampas. In Venezuela's Llanos area, ranches were worked by cowmen called *llaneros*.

Chilean huasos.

And cattle raising was carried out in Chile's Central Valley by men known as *huasos*. To a lesser degree, ranching was also established in Brazil, Colombia, and Uruguay.

Cattle raising became important to the economies of these countries, particularly those of Argentina, Chile, and Venezuela. And the cowmen in these nations became highly skilled.

exactly where the individual groups would be. Experienced vaqueros were also aware of which particular cows on their ranch were apt to stray and in which thicket or gullies they were most likely to be found.

Long after the glory days of both the vaqueros and the American cowboys had passed, a former cowhand put it this way: "I'll tell you what a cow puncher is," he wrote. "It ain't roping and it ain't riding bronc. . . . It's thinking enough about a dumb animal to go out in the rain or snow to try to save that cow. Not for the guy who owns the cow, but for the poor old cow and her calf. It's getting down in the bog. . . . You see this old cow, she doesn't know but what you're trying to kill her. But you drag her out, even if she's fighting you, and then you ride a mile yonder and find another danged old cow bogged down the same way." This passion for the well-being of the animals in their care was a noble trait. And it all began with the vaqueros.

The vaqueros fashioned much of the equipment they used themselves. The leather straps they made that went around their horses and kept their saddles from moving were fastened with metal rings and were called cinchas. To keep their booted feet firmly in place while mounted, the vaqueros created stirrups made of hollowed-out wood or leather. For protection against rocks and thorn-filled terrain, they covered the stirrups with wedge-shaped pieces of leather, which they named tapaderas ("toe fenders"). The star-shaped spurs, which were a distinguishing mark of the vaqueros, were attached to their boots by leather straps. Almost all this equipment was passed on to the American cowboys.

CHAPTER FOUR

THE VAQUEROS' SPECIAL SKILLS

HALF MAN, HALF HORSE

From the time he was a child, a vaquero was taught to ride. Visiting a mission ranch in Mexico the American author Richard Henry Dana saw a strange sight. "They are put upon a horse when only four or five years old, their little legs not long enough to come halfway over the sides." From that age on, vaqueros never stopped riding. Adult vaqueros at the same mission could "hardly go from one house to another without mounting a horse."

Being such great horsemen, vaqueros became almost a new type of person: a centaur who was only half there if he wasn't saddled up and riding. ["Vaqueros] on foot," stated Frederic Remington, "are odd fish.... Their knees work outward and they have a decided 'hitch' in their gait; but once let them get a foot in a stirrup and a grasp on the horn of the saddle, and a dynamite cartridge alone could expel them from their

The vaqueros could ride like the wind. They could also travel on horseback for hours on end. Perhaps their greatest riding skill, however, was their ability to quickly stop, start, and change directions no matter how difficult or dangerous the maneuver. In this illustration, a vaquero has brought his horse so close to a steer that they are actually touching. He will then easily be able to rope the animal and bring it under control.

seat. When loping over the plain the [vaquero] is the epitome of equine grace, and if he desires to look behind him he simply shifts his whole body to one side and lets the horse go as he pleases. In pursuit of cattle . . . he leans forward in his saddle . . . 'plugs' in his spurs and makes his pony fairly sail."

Vaqueros became great riders because their work demanded that of them. But they were just as ready to test their mounts and their skills by holding contests and playing death-defying games. *La sortija* (ring race) may originally have been part of a knight's training in medieval Spain. In America, it was open to all who could ride well enough. A horseman carrying a long wooden lance would ride madly toward a small golden ring that hung from a slender thread. The rider galloped at full speed, then dipped and drove his lance through its small opening without breaking stride. The first man to accomplish the difficult feat won the contest.

The vaqueros' favorite game was called *correr el gallo* (chicken race). No one would try this game today, but the vaqueros loved to play it. A chicken, duck, or rooster was buried up to its neck in the ground. Several vaqueros would then ride full tilt at the animal. The person who first succeeded in pulling the unfortunate bird from the earth would gallop off toward a distant finish line. The other vaqueros would take off in hot pursuit, determined to catch up with the man and grab the animal from him.

Like a massive game of tag on horseback, whoever had the bird would lead the other riders on endless cutbacks, crisscrosses, and other evasions across the open range. The vaquero who succeeded in crossing the finish line with animal in hand won the game.

A much tamer contest was called *recogiendo* (picking up). In this game, a small object such as a coin, a neckerchief, or an arrow was placed on the ground. A vaquero would ride very fast and lean down as far as he could, draping himself over the side of his horse without breaking stride. Calling for speed, courage, and great riding, the

The vaqueros' games gave them the opportunity to both test and show off their riding skills. Contests like correr el gallo (pictured here) dated back to the vaqueros' roots in Spain and remained with them through their days on the range both in Mexico and the United States.

game was a perfect showcase for vaqueros' skills. Fast-paced *recogiendo* contests were headline acts in the Wild West Shows that were so popular in America and across Europe in the late 1800s.

ROPING A TRAIN

Just as they were among the most accomplished of all horsemen, vaqueros were masters of the rope which they called a *reata*. "Without a rope," observed J. Frank Dobie, "the old time vaquero felt as lost as a hunter without a gun." On Mexican ranches a particularly skilled cowhand was often referred to as *un buen reata*, which literally means "a good rope."

Young vaqueros began handling ropes even before they started to ride. First, youngsters learned how to tie the knot that forms a *lazo* (lasso). Lassos are long ropes or leather thongs that end in a movable noose. They are perfect for catching a fleeing calf because you can throw the loop in a wide circle over the animal, then quickly pull it tight.

Once they mastered making lassos, vaqueros-in-training spent long hours practicing how to throw the ropes over a stationary object. Finally they faced the real challenge, roping an animal on the move.

Like all-star athletes today, there were vaqueros who became legendary for their feats with a rope. For example, some said that José Berrara, who in the 1870s and 1880s worked on both Mexican and American ranches on the Mexican–United States border, could rope just about any-

The vaquero's most important piece of equipment was his rope, called a reata. *Vaqueros made their own ropes out of a variety of materials. Some were made of woven horsehair. Others were constructed of the fibrous materials of the maguey plant, which grows in Mexico and in some parts of the American Southwest. Most of the vaqueros' ropes, however, were made by braiding strips of rawhide together.*

thing that moved, and he could do it faster than anyone had ever seen.

Vaqueros would test their skills by roping almost anything in front of them—dogs, chickens, fellow vaqueros. There were even reports, not totally confirmed, of vaqueros who lassoed birds in flight. Enough people claim to have seen a vaquero rope a railroad train that it probably happened.

In the hands of vaqueros, a lasso was a marvelous tool, and they gave special names to all the tricks they could make it perform. In order to bring down a running animal, for example, they invented the toss known as the figure

Vaqueros' ropes were made in different lengths to suit the purpose for which they were used. To avoid becoming tangled, shorter ropes were used when working in the brush. On the open range, as seen in this early drawing, much longer ropes were used.

eight. An underhand throw, called the *piale,* was the very best way to lasso a steer's hind legs. An overhead throw called the *mangana* was used to nab an animal's front legs.

The most important roping innovation the vaqueros brought to the range was developed shortly after they introduced the saddle horn. Called *dar la vuelta* (take a turn), the technique involved wrapping the rope used in lassoing a calf or steer tightly around the horn. This allowed the vaquero to gain important leverage against the animal once it was roped. Anyone who has been to a calf-roping event at a rodeo has seen this rapid-fire move completed in the split seconds before the rider leaps off his horse.

In this picture, the artist has clearly depicted the vaqueros' roping innovation called dar la vuelta. The vaquero has secured the lasso around the horse's neck by winding his rope tightly around his saddle horn. It seems like a simple technique, but before the vaqueros introduced the dar la vuelta method, roped animals often broke loose from their ropers, sometimes pulling them clear off their horses.

Wrapping a rope around the horn is very effective, yet it can also be dangerous. More than one vaquero lost his thumb when it got caught between the fast-moving rope and the saddle horn.

READING THE LAND

One of the most accomplished vaqueros was named Ignatio Flores. As a youngster he was captured by Comanches, who taught him how to track animals. Freed from captivity, he became a vaquero and put his special skill to work on an early Texas ranch. Flores had the ability to read nearly invisible signs that told him where to find missing cows, steers, and bulls. He was a kind of detective, a Sherlock Holmes of the range.

While following an animal's trail, Flores spent hours with his face inches from the ground. He discovered that blades of grass, stomped down by hooves, would start to spring back immediately and would continue to rise to their original position in three days. To his practiced eye, the angle of a blade of grass was a kind of timer, recording how long it had been since the creature he was trailing had passed by that exact spot.

Flores was alert to many kinds of clues. He found that studying the tiny marks made by insects crawling over a hoof print could tell a great deal about when the animal he was pursuing had been there. Carefully looking at the leaves a large animal pushed aside helped him to know which direction would be the most promising. Using these techniques Flores tracked down scores of animals that had been given up as lost.

Ignatio Flores was not the only vaquero specially skilled in the art of tracking. A vaquero with the single name of Tiburcio earned a reputation as being one of the best trackers in all the cattle country. Tiburcio, who worked on the Viejo Ranch in San Antonio during the 1870s and 1880s, could see a particular cow, steer, or bull, note its distinctive tracks, and then, as long as two years later, point out a track that he said was made by that one animal. More than once, when fellow vaqueros challenged his claim, Tiburcio took up the trail of the animal and proved that he was right.

Vaqueros did not limit their tracking to animals. J. Frank Dobie recalled the day he was about to leave the range to go off to college. He spent a lively afternoon on horseback trotting around with a group of cowmen. Together they traveled all around a brush-filled pasture covering some four thousand acres. When he returned to the ranch, Dobie discovered that one of his prized possessions, his pocket watch, was missing.

When he returned to the ranch Dobie told vaquero Genardo del Bosque about this frustrating loss. Asked where he had been riding, Dobie said sadly that he and his companions had been almost everywhere in the pasture, crisscrossing the same places several times. "Well," answered the confident vaquero, "I will take your trail and find the watch." An astonished Dobie asked if del Bosque could really tell the track of Dobie's horse from all the others that covered the pasture. "Sí, señor," was the vaquero's simple reply. Within hours of their conversation, Dobie, certain that his timepiece was gone forever, had to leave for college. He did not return until Christmas, some three months later. When he rode up to the ranch he was immediately greeted by del Bosque, who proudly presented him with his watch.

BREAKING, BUCKING, AND BRONCS

Most of the horses the vaqueros rode began their lives in the wild and had to be tamed or "broken." This was a difficult, dangerous task, and it required a very special man to do it. Known as *amansadores* (tamers), these vaqueros were paid extra, and they earned every *peso*.

The greatest difficulty in taming a wild horse was that each animal created its own brand of mayhem. Some leaped high into the air. Others bucked in circles or figure eights. Many twisted their bodies in midair, while some, after jumping off the ground, suddenly whirled backward. Among the most difficult to handle were those who simply charged straight forward and tried to drive themselves and their rider through fences or anything else that stood in their way.

Nestor Córdova was a man who moved from Mexico to the Avra Valley region in what is now Tucson, Arizona, in the early 1850s. He went to work on a ranch in that area and became an *amansador*. Over the years, he and his fellow tamers developed special ways of bringing the wild horses under control. They would usually begin by tying a long rope to the animal and letting it twist, turn, and buck for more than an hour, until it began to tire. Then they

Taming or "breaking" a wild horse required courage, skill, and no small amount of patience. Out of this adventurous, yet always dangerous, task came a number of cattle country expressions, originating in one form or another with the vaqueros. These expressions included, "Any man who says he's never been throwed is a liar," and "There's never been a horse that can't be rode; there's never been a cowman who hasn't been throwed."

would mount the horse. Sometimes they would blindfold the animal.

Other times they would tie their saddles to their horses. Whatever they did, they knew they were in for a rough ride. After weathering the first bucking session, which lasted for about two hours, *amansadores* such as Córdova would dismount and let the animal cool off. Then they would remount and go through the bucking act all over again. It usually took them five or six days of repeated mounting, bucking, and dismounting before a horse was tamed and ready to begin its work on the range.

No matter how skilled an *amansador* was, he was sure to be bucked off sometime, so he had to learn how to fall. When a trainer lost control, he would make his body go limp, then he'd hit the ground rolling, all while avoiding the slashing hooves of the animal. Still, many *amansadores* were injured and even killed. Few lasted more than ten years in their job, which was about all their bodies and their nerves could take.

Riding, roping, and bronco busting were special talents introduced and perfected by a special breed of men. As we attend today's rodeos, or have the opportunity to visit a modern ranch, we can still see the skills the vaqueros brought to the New World, and can perhaps catch a trace of vaquero heroes of long ago.

CHAPTER FIVE

VAQUEROS AT WORK: A PICTURE ESSAY

The vaqueros' working day began at sunup and often lasted well into the night. Their work life centered around meeting the many demands of tending the cattle on the range.

The highlight of the vaqueros' year was the spring roundup which lasted from three to four weeks. At the roundup, vaqueros from neighboring ranches came together to gather the herds and drive them to a central location. Calves that had been born since the last roundup and steers that had been purchased from other ranches were then separated from the herds and branded with the distinctive marking of each ranch.

The other great event in the vaqueros' life was the cattle drive in which they drove thousands of head of cattle over various trails to railroad yards far to the north. From there the cattle were taken by rail to slaughterhouses in meat-packing centers in distant cities such as Chicago.

The picture essay that follows shows the vaqueros conducting all these challenging tasks.

Range work involved continually rescuing steers and calves that had strayed and gotten themselves entrapped in the thicket that grew throughout the cattle country. It was a task that required the vaquero and his horse to work almost as one.

Vaqueros spent most of their time with the cattle on the open range, which stretched out for miles. Keeping track of the herds was a never-ending job.

One of the most spectacular sights of an early roundup was that of a vaquero in full gallop, madly waving his serape above his head as he drove a stray calf or steer back toward the herd. Worn over the shoulder like a shawl, the serape served the vaquero in several ways when he was out on the range. While tending the cattle on cold evenings, he wrapped it around himself as a jacket. When sleeping on the range, he used it as his bed. The most dramatic way in which the vaqueros used the serape, however, was as a tool for moving cattle along during the roundup.

This drawing, fanciful as it may be, depicts several aspects of the roundup. Vaqueros in a semicircle formation have gathered the herd together and have driven it forward. One of the steers, targeted for branding, has been separated or "cut" from the herd. The animal has been roped by a vaquero astride a specially trained roping horse and will soon be dragged off to a branding area. In the foreground of the picture sits the chuck wagon, an important part of every roundup, out of which the cook prepared and served meals to the cowhands.

The earliest cattle drives were those carried out by vaqueros who trailed herds to posts along the Gulf of Mexico. When the vaqueros joined the cowboys on American ranches, they became key members of much longer trail drives. In 1872, V. F. Carbajal, Miguel Cantu, Macedonio Gortari, Melchior Jimenez, Aurielio Carbajal, Juan Bueno, Anastacio Sanchez, Francisco Longoria, and a vaquero cook made up the entire outfit that successfully drove fifteen hundred steers from Texas to Nebraska guided only by a compass and a crude map.

This drawing of vaqueros driving Texas cattle to market in New Orleans appeared in Harper's Weekly in 1867. One of the toughest challenges of the trail drive was getting the cattle across the many rivers along the way. Cattle were afraid of water, and it was hard enough to get them across calm rivers. When the rivers were swollen by melted snow or torrential rains, every crossing became treacherous.

The greatest danger of any trail drive came from stampedes. Vaqueros became known for the courage they displayed in racing after a stampede herd, chasing it for miles, and finally bringing it under control.

CHAPTER SIX

TALES OF THE VAQUEROS

TUG-OF-WAR WITH A BEAR

The vaqueros were great storytellers. They loved to recount old stories, weave new tales, and listen to yarns spun by their companions. Most of these stories were told at night when the day's work was done and the vaqueros gathered around the evening campfire. Some told of heroic vaquero deeds, while others painted word pictures of legendary bandits, described gleaming piles of buried treasure, or warned of mysterious or supernatural happenings. Not only are these vaquero tales fascinating stories, but they show us a great deal about the vaqueros and the world in which they lived.

One of the favorite stories was that of a vaquero named Pablo Romero and his encounter with an amazing animal. According to the tale, a bear once ate a vaquero who had

In this drawing, the artist captured in the faces of the men the way in which va-queros were held spellbound by tales told when the day's work was done. Those vaqueros who were particularly skilled at storytelling were held in high regard.

attempted to capture him. The bear was called Star Breast because of the star-shaped white spot on his chest. He liked the taste of the vaquero so much that he started lying in wait for other men. The bear was spotted many times. But even though hunters shot at him, no bullet could bring him down. Within a short time, Star Breast became so well known for the number of people he carried off and devoured that no one would go near his hideout.

Still, there was a young man named Pablo Romero, whose great desire was to be regarded as the bravest of all the vaqueros. One day while Romero and another vaquero were tracking down some wild horses, they came across tracks that Romero knew were those of Star Breast. Without hesi-tation, Romero announced that he was going to kill the bear.

He told his companions that since it seemed useless to try to shoot the animal, and since using a gun instead of a rope was a sign of cowardice anyway, he was going to throw a lasso around the bear's neck and choke him to death.

Romero's fellow vaquero was truly alarmed. He urged his friend to give up what he felt was a foolhardy idea. But Romero would not listen. "A good roper, a good roping horse, and a good *reata*," he said, "can conquer anything."

Romero's companion reluctantly agreed to stay with him but only if he could watch the roping from a distance. The two men followed Star Breast's tracks until they led them to

It was not surprising that the grizzly bear was the subject of different vaquero tales. The grizzly was one of the most ferocious of all animals. It could break the neck of a full-grown steer with a single blow from its paw. Almost as soon as the earliest vaqueros went to work on the Spanish missions in California, they found that keeping grizzlies from attacking and killing the cattle they tended was one of their greatest challenges.

a thicket. Suddenly the huge animal appeared. Standing on his hind legs, he gave out an ear-splitting roar and charged at Romero.

The vaquero quickly fastened one end of his *reata* to his saddle. He then threw the rope over the bear's head while his horse dug its hooves into the ground. Star Breast pulled mightily against the rope and struggled to keep standing. Several times he was jerked down, but the rope had slipped from the bear's neck to under one of its arms. Perhaps if the rope had stayed around Star Breast's neck, Romero would have indeed been able to choke him. But that was not the case.

As the struggle continued, Star Breast attempted to bite through the rope under its arm. Romero responded by giving a gigantic tug on the *reata*. As one of the bear's teeth fell to the ground, it gave out its mightiest roar of all. Star Breast spat out the rope and grabbed the *reata* with its huge paws. Slowly but surely the gigantic bear began to work its way up the rope toward Romero. As Star Breast got closer, the vaquero tried desperately to pull the *reata* out of the bear's paws. But the rope was wound so tightly around the saddle that the vaquero could not cut it loose.

If Romero's companion had been as courageous as Romero, he might have been able to throw his own *reata* over the bear. But he was truly frightened. All he could do was look on in terror. What he saw next was incredible.

As Star Breast reached Romero and his horse, he dragged the vaquero from his saddle. The bear then took the rope off his neck, wound it up, and tied it to the saddle horn. Then he mounted the vaquero's horse. With Romero lying across the saddle before him, Star Breast galloped off into the deep thicket. No one ever saw the vaquero or his horse again.

The story of Pablo Romero and Star Breast was a fable. But like many vaquero tales it is based on one of their actual activities. Vaqueros in California regularly engaged in a most unusual and dangerous sport. Several vaqueros would seek out a grizzly bear and would lasso it by the neck and feet. The rope around the bear's neck would cut off enough air to subdue the animal. The vaqueros would then untie the rope around the bear's feet and lead it back to the ranch.

It is clear why vaqueros would enjoy the telling and retelling of Pablo Romero and Star Breast. Courage, even if it was foolhardy at times, was always admired. And vaqueros particularly appreciated the fact that Romero attempted to conquer the grizzly with a rope instead of a gun.

The story also gave those vaqueros who listened to it the opportunity to voice their displeasure with Romero's companion. Not coming to the aid of a fellow vaquero, especially at a time of danger, was regarded as the most despicable of all human traits. The ending of the story, in which the grizzly takes on human qualities in subduing and riding off with Romero, undoubtedly appealed to the vaqueros' sense of humor and their enjoyment of tales with a supernatural twist.

THE REAL HEADLESS HORSEMAN

The story of Pablo Romero was undoubtedly made up. Another that sounds like the famous story set in Sleepy Hollow may actually have been true. It is the tale of the headless horseman of the mustangs.

In the 1850s, people living along the Nueces River in what is now Texas reported seeing a wild black mustang stallion carrying on his back a horseman without a head. Those who witnessed this ghostly rider said that he carried his head under a sombrero with a pure gold band. Both head and sombrero were tied to the stallion's saddle horn.

As time went on, more and more sightings of this headless horseman were reported. There seemed to be no particular time or place when the mustang and rider would suddenly appear. Those who saw it swore that it was the fastest horse that had ever raced across the range. Neither the animal nor its rider ever appeared to get tired, and witnesses reported that no matter how fast they rode, the headless figure never bent down or looked around, but remained perfectly rigid as if nailed to the saddle.

This weird sight terrified both man and beast. When other mustangs spotted it, they ran off in alarm. It was said that the one sure signal that the headless horseman was in the area was the sight of a herd of wild mustangs racing off in fright.

Even the Indians in the region, who were constantly hunting wild horses, were terrified of the mustang and its rider and raced off in alarm whenever they encountered them. Vaqueros, those bravest of men, were also scared.

According to the story, the stallion and the headless horseman were never captured and continued to strike fear into the hearts of all who saw them long after the last vaquero had left the range.

Like many of the tales the vaqueros told, this story of the headless horseman had several versions. Vaqueros who preferred tales of ghosts and other supernatural creatures saw no need to question this tale. Others who sought an explanation for all things that seemed mysterious preferred the following version:

During the mid-1800s, a Mexican known as Vidal was the leader of a band of horse thieves who operated along the Mexico-Texas border. In the summer of 1859, Vidal and his men raided a Texas ranch and made off with a large group of horses. Some of the horses that were stolen belonged to Creed Taylor, a man who was not the type of person to let his property be stolen without doing everything possible to get it back.

A Mexican rancher named Flores had also lost horses in Vidal's raid. He agreed to join Taylor in pursuing the horse thieves and getting back their animals. As they followed the trail of the robbers, Taylor and Flores met up with Bigfoot Wallace, a man who was always ready for an adventure, particularly if it included a good fight. Wallace happily joined in the pursuit.

Somewhere along the Nueces River, the men spotted smoke from a campfire. Silently they made their way to the camp and decided to wait until nightfall to act. When darkness came, Taylor crept forward to get a better look. Immediately he spotted the stolen horses. Crawling closer, Taylor then saw one man on guard while three others lay asleep.

Vaquero Music

Vaquero music and storytelling were related. Like the vaqueros' stories, many of their songs were based on the type of work they did and the challenges they faced. One of the vaqueros' favorite songs, for example, was titled "Mi Caballo Bayo" (my bay horse) and told the story of a vaquero who loved his horse so much that he refused to sell him even when he was offered a huge price. Another typical vaquero song, titled "El Toro Moro" (the Moorish bull), celebrated an especially courageous and terrifying bull.

A vaquero band.

Other vaquero songs recounted the deeds of bold Mexican outlaw heroes such as Gregorio Cortés and Hercal Bernal who were regarded as Mexican Robin Hoods. Perhaps the most popular type of song was that in which a vaquero lamented the loss of a sweetheart. Rough-and-ready as the vaqueros were, they sang these and other types of love songs over and over again.

The vaqueros introduced the guitar and several other smaller related string instruments to the range. Much of their singing was done amidst the herds. This was particularly true at night, a time when the cattle often got restless and were easily spooked. The vaqueros discovered early on that soft, steady singing helped to keep the cattle from becoming startled by unexpected evening sounds.

One of these men he identified as Vidal. Returning to his comrades, Taylor came up with a plan. He and Wallace would creep up next to the sleeping bandits. Flores would hide in a nearby thicket and wait until the man on guard walked past him. Flores would then shoot the guard. Upon hearing the shot, Taylor and Wallace would then do away with the other thieves.

The plan went off almost without a fault. Flores fired at his man. When they heard the shot, Taylor and Wallace used their six-shooters to kill the other three bandits as they tried to struggle to their feet. The only hitch was that Flores's target was only wounded and managed to get away.

When daylight broke, Wallace figured out what to do next. He knew that among the recaptured horses there was a black stallion that had never been saddled. The imaginative Wallace suggested that he rope and saddle the horse, mount Vidal's body upon it, and turn it loose. This, he said, would serve as a dire warning to all other horse thieves. Then the ranchers came up with an even wilder scheme. They dressed Vidal's body in a buckskin jacket, leggings, and *serape,* and tied his feet to the saddle's stirrups so that it could not fall off. Then they placed a sombrero on top of the dead horse thief's head and cut the head from Vidal's body. Finally, they tied the head securely to the saddle horn.

The smell of the blood from Vidal's severed head drove the already wild stallion thoroughly mad. First it raised up on its hind legs, then with nostrils flaring, it gave out an enormous squeal. Finally, it raced off into the distance at a speed faster than any of the ranchers had ever seen a horse gallop.

According to this version of the story, sightings of the headless horseman began almost immediately afterward. Finally a group of frontiersmen came upon the mustang as it was drinking from the Nueces. On its back they discovered the bullet-ridden, dried-up body of a Mexican. The man's head, covered with a sombrero, was lashed to his saddle horn. At last there was an explanation to the mystery of the headless horseman.

The land on which the vaqueros lived and worked provided a natural setting for their belief in the supernatural. The howling, ghost-sounding winds that constantly whipped across the open range, the dark foreboding hills that loomed over the prairie, the many pitch-black evenings that the vaqueros spent guarding the cattle, and the sounds of wild animals shrieking in the night all contributed to their belief in strange forces and their appreciation of stories like that of the headless horseman.

EL TEJANO

Stories such as that of three ranchers' revenge on those who had stolen their horses had special meaning for the vaqueros. They depended almost totally on their horses for their livelihood and considered horse thieves the lowest form of humanity. As far as the vaqueros were concerned, no punishment was too severe for a person who stole another man's horse.

There were, however, other types of bandits whom the vaqueros admired. These included Robin Hood types who stole from the rich and gave their plunder to the poor. This is the story the vaqueros told about El Tejano, the Texan.

El Tejano was a bandit who concentrated on robbing stagecoaches in what is now Arizona. After hiding the riches that he stole, he would bury them and then dig them up when he felt it was safe to do so. Then he would distribute the valuable items among those who barely had enough money to buy food.

One of El Tejano's favorite targets was the stagecoach running on a road that wound among the foothills of a mountain called El Cerro del Gato (Cat Back Mountain). Since this particular stagecoach carried gold and silver coins which mine and ranch owners used to pay their workers, it always traveled with at least one armed guard aboard. Despite this, El Tejano succeeded in robbing the stagecoach several times.

El Tejano was among the most clever of all bandits in the vaquero territory. One of his favorite tricks was accomplished through the aid of a blacksmith named Don Cayetano. Before setting out to rob a stagecoach, El Tejano would take his horse to Cayetano's shop. There the blacksmith would put the animal's horseshoes on backward. When lawmen tried to follow El Tejano after he had robbed a coach, they would always pursue the bandit in the wrong direction.

One day, however, El Tejano was betrayed. Someone warned a sheriff and his deputies that the southwestern Robin Hood was about to rob the stagecoach once again. The informer even identified the exact spot where the robbery was to take place. When El Tejano arrived, the lawmen

One of the stories that the vaqueros loved to tell was that of Joaquín Murieta, a Mexican outlaw who, in the early 1850s, protected Mexican maidens from abuse and who robbed rich Americans and gave his plunder to the poor. Murieta's story was printed in newspapers and magazines. Paintings of him, like this one, were created, and a popular song was written about him. A respected history text included his story. He became celebrated throughout the world, particularly in Spain. But Joaquín Murieta never existed. He and his story had originally been made up by author John Ridge in a book titled The Life and Adventures of Joaquín Murieta, Celebrated California Bandit. It is a prime example of how a story is created, grows over time, and then becomes accepted as fact.

The ritual of the nightly storytelling session around the evening campfire was yet another contribution the vaqueros made to the American cowboys. Through the stories they told, the vaqueros supplied the cowboys with the basis for many of the yarns they spun.

were waiting for him and without hesitation shot him dead. Those who knew El Tejano were sure there were still hoards of buried treasure that the bandit had not had time to recover. Since it was widely believed that the riches were hidden somewhere in the earth of El Cerro del Gato, scores of people began climbing the mountain in search of the treasures, but none was ever found. Perhaps, recounted the vaqueros in their telling of the story, this was because the ghost of El Tejano, astride his horse, protected the booty and frightened off anyone who came close to the sites of the treasure.

The story of El Tejano was but one of several vaquero tales of the deeds of famous Mexican bandits. It was particularly popular because in El Tejano's personal qualities the vaqueros found characteristics they greatly admired. Because they were often victims of Anglo-American racial prejudice and because they were paid less than their white cowboy counterparts, vaqueros loved stories of men who risked their lives to take from the American rich in order to give to the Mexican poor.

The vaqueros also admired the clever way in which the outnumbered El Tejano evaded his pursuers for so long. At the same time, possessing a sense of fate that was a strong vaquero characteristic, most of them understood the inevitability of the bandit finally losing out to a greater force. The fact that the story ends with the ghost of El Tejano still protecting the buried treasure provided the vaqueros with yet another example of supernatural forces at work.

CHAPTER SEVEN

THE VAQUERO BECOMES INVISIBLE

BARBED WIRE AND BAD WINDS

By the 1880s, cattle raising in the United States had become an immense industry. Over 1.3 million square miles of land were devoted to raising cattle. That was 44 percent of all the land in the United States. Yet before another decade was over, the glory days of life on the range came to an end.

There were several reasons for this dramatic turn of events. Beginning in the late 1840s, millions of Americans, seeking new opportunities and better lives, began making the long and terribly difficult journey from cities and towns in the eastern part of the nation to the sparsely settled West. They were encouraged by the United States government, which gave them hundreds of acres of free land in exchange for their promise to farm their new property.

By the late 1870s, these farmers were planting crops

As the United States entered the last quarter of the 1800s, the look of the American range began to change dramatically. Whereas artists of the West had earlier portrayed scenes in which horses, longhorns, and cowmen filled the landscape, their drawings now often showed covered wagons and pioneers making their way to the western lands.

throughout the western lands. They also raised sheep, cows, horses, and other animals. Aided by the recent invention of barbed wire, they protected their crops and livestock by erecting long fences around their property. By doing so, they increasingly closed off the open range, which had for so long been the lifeblood of the cattle industry.

In the years after the Civil War, railroads stretched further and further into the West. Now more and more people could easily leave their homes and light out to create new farms. As each family moved west it cut one more piece out of the open range. And as new tracks and stations brought trains into cattle country, there was less and less need for long trail drives. The animals could now be herded onto railroad cars wherever they grazed, and could then be taken directly to the slaughterhouses. The shorter the drives and the smaller the range, the less need for vaqueros and cowboys.

The 1880s brought the final act in the story of the cow-men. The first problem was success: there were so many cows that prices for beef kept dropping. For the first time, raising cows was a way to lose money.

"The changes now taking place [in the United States]," proclaimed future President James Garfield in 1873, *"have been wrought and are being wrought mainly, almost wholly, by a single mechanical contrivance, the steam locomotive. The railway is the greatest centralizing force of modern times."* As trains brought millions of settlers into the western territories, and as railroad tracks became a common sight on cattle ranges, new ways of life were beginning and old ways were soon to fade.

Then came the weather. In 1886, the cattle country experienced the most severe winter the region had ever known. As unrelenting winds blew day after day, and as the temperature in many areas dropped to 30 and 40 degrees below zero, cattle died by the hundreds of thousands. Of the 5,500 head of cattle on one Texas ranch, for example, only one hundred survived. In Wyoming alone, 250,000 animals lost their lives. To even the most die-hard cattlemen, the winter of 1886 proved to be the last straw.

OFF THE RANGE AND ONTO THE SCREEN

Even as the real work of the cowmen was coming to an end, cowboys were being turned into legends. As it became increasingly clear that these ropers and riders were about to vanish from the scene, a flood of books, magazines, and stage plays celebrating their exploits began to appear. Just as the West became a place of farmers, trains, and small towns, the Wild West was born. In shows, on stages, in plays, and later in the movies, on radio, and on television, cowboys rode the range.

In all these heroic portrayals there were no vaqueros. The stories were all about white American cowboys. The vaqueros' courage, loyalty, and skills had enabled them to create the art of cattle raising. They had invented the American cowboy by teaching him almost all they knew. During the cowboy's glory days, vaqueros still made up over half the workforce on most Texas and southwestern ranches. Yet they were totally missing from the pages of the books and the scripts of the stage plays.

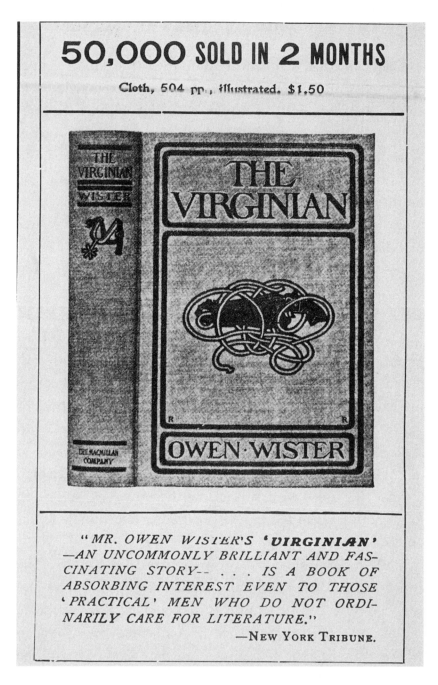

50,000 SOLD IN 2 MONTHS

Cloth, 504 pp., illustrated. $1.50

"MR. OWEN WISTER'S 'VIRGINIAN' —AN UNCOMMONLY BRILLIANT AND FASCINATING STORY-- . . . IS A BOOK OF ABSORBING INTEREST EVEN TO THOSE 'PRACTICAL' MEN WHO DO NOT ORDINARILY CARE FOR LITERATURE."
—NEW YORK TRIBUNE.

The Virginian, *written by Owen Wister and published in 1902, was very popular. The book, which became a model for hundreds of similar works and was made into a movie, contained not a single word about cattle and not even a mention of a vaquero.*

As the number of literary and stage depictions of the cowmen rapidly increased, the vaquero remained invisible. Why was this so? The main reason was that these portrayals were created at a time of deep racial and ethnic prejudice in the United States. At the turn of the century, violence against African-Americans rose to all-time highs. Prejudiced people were determined to prevent them from truly claiming the rights they had earned during the Civil War.

This atmosphere of intolerance was intensified by the presence of millions of immigrants who were pouring into the nation from countries around the world. As the United States became increasingly filled with people with different-colored skin, many of whom spoke "strange" languages, some residents reacted with hostility and hatred. They longed for someone they could regard as a true American hero. And they found that hero in the white American cowboy.

The few books and magazines that did mention vaqueros did so in a totally distorted way. Vaqueros were called "untrustworthy," "unlikeable," "lazy," and even "debauched"—that is, corrupted by their weakness for women and liquor.

For example, Colonel Theodore A. Dodge wrote this in an 1891 issue of *Harper's New Monthly Magazine:* "The vaquero is . . . lazy, shiftless, and unreliable. . . . He is essentially a low down fellow in his habits and instinct. . . . Our cowboy . . . has as long an array of manly qualities as any fellow living, and despite many rough-and-tumble traits compels our honest admiration. . . . The percentage of American cowboys who are not pretty decent fellows is small. One cannot claim so much for the vaquero."

Plays also ignored the accomplishments of the vaqueros. This poster, advertising a stage play of the time, depicts a typical ending for books and plays of the West. The cowboy has slain the villain who was menacing the beautiful young woman, and true love is his reward.

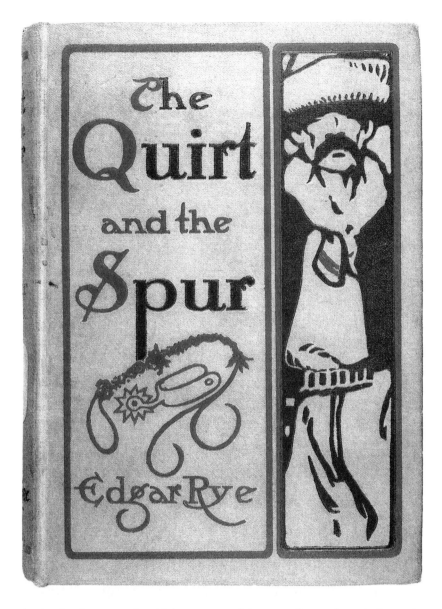

In the few instances in which vaqueros did appear in novels and plays, they were depicted in a manner in keeping with the racial prejudice they often experienced. Typical of this type of portrayal was the cover of this early novel of the West. The title was taken from two items of equipment that the vaqueros introduced to American cattle raising (a quirt was a flexible leather whip sometimes used to urge on an uncooperative horse). Yet the vaquero, with his dark foreboding mustache and sinister expression, was portrayed as a dangerous individual, a man not to be trusted, and unlike the cowboy, not to be admired.

Anyone who had spent any time with vaqueros or who had worked alongside them knew that Dodge's portrayal was entirely false. Yet with few exceptions, the vaqueros continued to be either ignored in the stories of the cowmen or turned into villains or fools.

And it was not just in books, magazines, and stage plays that they were invisible. Despite the extraordinary accomplishments of vaqueros such as Faustina Villa, Nestor Córdova, V. F. Carbajal, Juan Reón, Eli Lucero, and scores of others, only one vaquero was ever elected to the National Cowboy Hall of Fame established in Oklahoma City, Oklahoma, in 1965. His name was Ramón Ahumada. During his almost fifty years on the range, he earned a reputation among both fellow vaqueros and the cowboys with whom he worked as one of the greatest of all cowmen. His skill as a horseman was perhaps exceeded only by his ability with a rope. An expert tracker, he was also one of the few vaqueros who was ever elevated to the position of foreman on an American ranch. His presence in the National Cowboy Hall of Fame is fully deserved. But where are the others?

Although the vaqueros were unheralded and even ignored, the public did see pictures of them and the work they performed. But no one knew what they were looking at. Many of the books that celebrated the cowboy contained illustrations. Often, the pictures included in these books depicted vaqueros rather than cowboys.

The vaqueros' appearance both in book illustrations and in advertisements had nothing to do with publishers and advertisers attempting to give them their place in the story of the range. It had everything to do with the publishers and

In this photograph we see Ramón Ahumada, the only vaquero ever inducted into the National Cowboy Hall of Fame. Standing beside him is his young nephew. One of the most skilled of all cowmen, Ahumada was particularly admired for his encyclopedic knowledge of almost every brand on the range.

advertisers using images of the vaqueros for their own commercial purposes. There was, however, another type of commercial venture through which the vaqueros, without false identity, gained a measure of public visibility. It was called the Wild West Show.

This drawing, titled Cow Boy, *is typical of the way in which books about the cowboys were illustrated with pictures not of cowboys but of vaqueros. Perhaps this was because the clothing of the vaqueros was far more colorful than that of the cowboys. Whatever the reason, time and again an illustration labeled "An American Cowboy" or "A Cowboy in Action" was really that of a vaquero.*

The Wild West Show was the invention of a man named William F. Cody. A former buffalo hunter and frontier scout, Cody was also an accomplished self-promoter and showman who called himself Buffalo Bill. In 1882, he came up with an idea that he believed would increase his fame and earn him a fortune. He decided to create an enormous show that would feature spectacular demonstrations of all the cowmen's skills, and would include enactments of real and fictionalized stagecoach robberies and made-up battles between cowboys and Indians.

As the cowboy continued to attain superhero status, advertisers, always anxious to identify their products with a popular figure, began using images of the cowboys in their ads. But, as in the book illustrations, it was not pictures of cowboys that were drawn, but visual portrayals of vaqueros. There was a reason. What better way to illustrate the dependability of a product being advertised than identifying it with the strength of a vaquero's piece of equipment such as his reata? And what better way to attract attention to the ad than featuring the vaqueros' colorful attire?

BUFFALO BIL
AND CONGRESS OF ROU

A COMPANY OF WILD WEST COWBOY

From its first performance in 1883 until its last in 1916, Buffalo Bill's Wild West Show was one of the nation's greatest attractions. People flocked to witness the feats of the cowmen about whom they had read so much. William Cody announced the coming of each show with large, colorful posters pasted throughout the city or town where his extravaganza was to take place. Al-

S WILD WEST
RIDERS OF THE WORLD.

COL.W.F.CODY
"BUFFALO BILL"
WILL APPEAR
AT EVERY PERFORMANCE

COPYRIGHT 1899
COURIER
LITHO.CO.
BUFFALO

EAL ROUGH RIDERS OF THE WORLD WHOSE DARING EXPLOITS
MADE THEIR VERY NAMES SYNONYMOUS WITH DEEDS OF BRAVERY.

most all these posters featured depictions of the vaqueros who, as members of the "Congress of Rough Riders of the World," headlined the show. Notice how the vaquero in the center foreground of the poster is demonstrating the skill involved in the vaquero contest known as picking-up.

In the westerns, the main characters were always white, handsome American cowboys who spent their days not with cattle but in performing amazing deeds such as shooting Indians from the tops of canyons, battling bad guys in black hats on the roofs of fast-moving trains, or saving beautiful women in distress.

Although above all else William F. Cody was a showman, he was not interested in glorifying the cowboy at the expense of the vaquero. From his own observations, he was aware of the vaqueros' abilities and he knew how much their presence would add to his show. From the beginning, he included such outstanding vaquero horsemen as Antonio Esquival and such renowned ropers as José Berrara.

These men and other vaqueros whom Cody hired so thrilled his audiences that, early on, he made an important addition to his extravaganza. He gathered together a large

The most unjust aspect of westerns went beyond the simple absence of the vaqueros in meaningful roles. With the exception of the 1990s movie Zorro, in which the main character was a positive, heroic Hispanic figure, vaqueros who did appear were shown in the worst possible light. In those films, for example, where the main character had a vaquero sidekick, that vaquero was always depicted as a bumbling, comic figure. In other movies, vaqueros were cast as heartless, unattractive, smirking bandits, the target of the cowboys' (and the audience's) wrath.

group of specially skilled vaqueros, gave the group the name "Congress of Rough Riders of the World," and made it a featured attraction. The feats of riding and roping that these men performed not only became the show's greatest attraction, but brought attention to at least some of the vaqueros.

But any gains vaqueros made from appearing in Buffalo Bill's Wild West Show were soon lost. A whole new form of entertainment made sure of that. It was called motion pictures, or later on more commonly the movies, and it quickly became the most popular form of entertainment the nation had ever known.

Of all the subjects of these early motion pictures, films about the cowboys became the most popular by far. Through these movies, called westerns, the cowboy became an even greater hero.

The fact that the vaqueros became almost invisible at the same time that the cowboys were being glorified was not simply unjust to them. It was unfair to all those interested in the truth. Failing to recognize who the vaqueros were and what they did robbed the pages of history of one of its most colorful and vital stories. For without the vaqueros, the saga of the American West is seriously incomplete.

CHAPTER EIGHT

COWMEN TODAY

It has been more than one hundred years since the days of the great cattle drives. Gone are the enormous thundering herds, the seemingly endless open range, and the mounted men who used their mustangs as tools to bring the cows safely home. In the minds of many people, the cowman, too, has long since vanished. But although cattle raising and life on the range have changed dramatically, they have far from disappeared.

Throughout today's cattle country, cowhands still ride the range tending calves and steers, mending fences, and recovering stray animals. There are still roundups, complete with brandings. And, as has been the case for more than two centuries, vaqueros still stand at the core of the operations of many of the ranches in the Southwest.

Most of these ranches are very different in appearance from those of the last decades of the 1800s. With the excep-

Although today's breeds of cattle are not as ornery as the fabled longhorns, many of the challenges of ranching are the same today as those of earlier times. Despite the aid of many technological advances and machines, the skills of riding and roping, introduced by the vaqueros, are still essential to the work of the ranch.

tion of legendary spreads like the King and Kenedy ranches, few stretch for more than one thousand acres (about 1.5 square miles). Most contain less than a thousand cattle. This reduction in size, along with many technological advancements in the art of raising cattle, has also reduced the number of cowhands required on each cattle spread. Most of today's ranches usually employ about ten full-time cowmen along with part-timers who are brought in for special occasions like the roundup.

On modern ranches, pickup trucks have become as common as corrals and watering troughs. Pickups, for example, have spelled the end of the chuck wagon, long one of the

Vaqueros continue to be tied to the land and the cattle in a relationship that has gone on for more than two centuries. This modern vaquero carries out many of the same tasks as his ancestors. And just as earlier vaqueros passed on their skills to the cowboys, he and his fellow modern vaqueros do the same for young people today.

trademarks of the cowman's way of life. Today's vaqueros and cowboys, both on the range and during the roundup, have their meals delivered to them by pickup wherever they are working.

The most dramatic example of the way in which technology has changed life on the range has been the increased presence of helicopters. One of the most common uses of this marvel of the air age has been its employment in locating stray cattle and steers. From his vantage point, a helicopter pilot can easily spot any animal that has gotten itself entangled in a thicket or stranded in a high-sided gully.

On today's ranches, pickup trucks are used for a variety of purposes. In areas of the range where grass is sparse, they carry bales of hay to the animals. During fence-mending operations, pickups towing horse vans are used to transport men and their mounts to the far reaches of the ranch. In this picture, Rene Martínez, a member of a vaquero family, has used a pickup to bring equipment to a branding crew.

Through the use of a two-way radio, the pilot can then direct mounted cowhands to the animal.

Helicopters are also often used to head off disasters. Chito Mendietta is a modern vaquero whose family has worked for generations on the Kenedy Ranch. "Our use of helicopters," says Mendietta, "came about because there was a fever tick in the middle of the 1970s, and we had to gather all the cattle in fourteen days and dip them. We couldn't do it on horseback so we got the helicopters. It's a lot faster. We began contracting with helicopter companies. Before helicopters, it took about fifteen [cowhands] a week to gather a pasture of three or four hundred cows. We

On many of today's ranches the sight of a helicopter rounding up cattle is as common as the old-time spectacle of the animals being driven forward by serape-waving vaqueros.

would ride horses from one end to the other, gather them in groups, then start penning them in . . . 'til we had them gathered. With three helicopters we can gather a six-thousand-acre pasture in about three hours."

The use of helicopters has proven particularly valuable during roundup time. Today's roundups combine almost all the techniques introduced by the vaqueros with innovations made possible by modern inventions. As in the earlier times, the first task of the roundup is to gather the herds together and move them to a central location. On many ranches the

In this picture we can see the way in which many of the techniques introduced by the vaqueros are still employed. At the top of the picture, a modern vaquero astride a cutting horse is separating from the herd a calf to be branded. At the bottom of the picture a branding crew places the ranch's distinctive mark on an animal. They are aided by the mounted vaquero to the right, who with his skilled roping horse keeps the animal secured during the branding operation.

cattle are driven forward not only by cowhands on horseback but by the noise from low-flying helicopters.

There have also been significant changes in the way the cattle are branded. The early vaqueros built their branding fires using the roots of the mesquite plant. Today's branding crews either heat their irons on burners fueled by propane gas or use irons that are electrically heated. The crews include men who vaccinate the cattle to protect them from disease.

Thanks to computers, cattle breeding, once a hit-or-miss process, has become an almost exact science. Through the use of computers, modern ranchers can learn the genetic characteristics of each of their cows and bulls and can use this information to mate those animals which have the best chance of producing offspring that will be healthy and will contain the highest quality of beef.

Computers have also changed the way many ranch owners buy and sell their animals. Today there are companies that videotape cattle and horses for sale. Ranchers tune in to a special livestock channel and carry out their transactions over the Internet.

With all these advances, however, today's ranch owners operate under extremely difficult conditions. Much of this is caused by the continual drops in the prices that owners receive for the cattle they raise. Much of it is also due to changes in Americans' eating habits. In the last two decades, countless people have adopted the belief that eating too much beef is bad for you. Fewer sales of beef in the supermarkets means fewer sales of cattle to meat packagers.

Despite these serious challenges, there are ranch owners and cowmen determined to carry on the ranching tradition.

Although by the end of the 1800s the glory days of the cowmen were over, thousands of vaqueros continued to work ranches throughout the cattle country. In this photograph, taken in 1930, vaquero Andres Robles races across the La Mota Ranch in La Salle County, Texas.

It is in their blood. The majority of the workforce of today's King and Kenedy ranches, for example, is made up of vaquero families, many of whom have been the backbone of the ranches for five or six generations. King Ranch vaqueros such as Rogerio Silva can still boast that they have ridden more than five hundred thousand miles on a horse.

Many modern vaqueros are highly educated. Men like Lin Becerra hold college degrees in such subjects as animal science and quality management. As ranch unit managers, they use their knowledge to make certain that efficient management is as much a part of the ranch's operations as are cutting out the herds and rounding up the strays.

Chito Mendietta, Rogerio Silva, Lin Becerra, and all the other modern vaqueros follow a proud tradition. They and those who came before them have been instrumental in making ranching a vital part of the American story. But far more than we realize, we have been affected by them in much deeper ways. They have profoundly influenced the way we talk, how we dress, the food we eat, the products we buy, and the things we hold important.

Some of our favorite proverbs, for example, come from the vaqueros. Among them are such phrases as "Appearances are deceiving," "Don't make trouble if you don't

Among the many things inherited from the vaqueros' fondness for demonstrating their riding and roping skills is the rodeo. In modern times the rodeo has become one of America's most popular attractions. Through the television screen in particular, millions of people have come into contact with those feats of daring and skill introduced by the vaqueros long before the viewers' grandparents and even great-grandparents were born.

want trouble," and "Misfortune, like the rattler, does not always give warning."

A great many of our most commonly used expressions come directly from the vaqueros as well. When we express our confidence in a particular undertaking by saying "it's a cinch," we are using an expression related to the piece of equipment that held a vaquero's saddle securely in place. When we "spur someone on," we are stating a phrase related to another piece of vaquero equipment. By telling one of our friends "not to let it throw you," we are, without realizing it, using a modified version of the advice vaqueros gave to their fellows when they mounted a bucking bronco.

When we say that something is "earmarked" for a particular use, we are employing a term that has its origins in one of the vaqueros' methods of identifying a steer or calf as belonging to their ranch. If we suggest that some of our friends "keep their ears to the ground," we are using an expression that originated in the Indian and vaquero practice of literally putting an ear to the earth to anticipate the approach of a herd of cattle or horses.

Other commonly used expressions that we owe to the vaqueros include: "Give him the boot," "Don't stampede me into it," "I'm being kept out of the loop," "He's got to be reined in," "Don't let her corral you," "I've got to take the bit in my mouth," and "I refuse to be branded in that way."

The vaqueros' influence is all around us. Over the years car makers have given names like Mustang and Bronco to their automobiles. Millions of Americans delight in eating tortillas, burritos, and tacos, all favorite dishes of the

"The American public," historian Carolina Castillo Grimm has written, "never knew that vaqueros . . . really were the true cowboys, quiet, hard-working, honest, faithful, law-abiding men with courage, stamina, tremendous skill, and a lack of fear." We owe them much. And one thing is for certain. As long as people desire beef, there will be cattle ranches. And as long as there are cattle ranches, there will be vaqueros.

vaqueros. The boots, the wide-brimmed hats, and the guitar music we enjoy all have their roots in vaquero culture.

But what we owe most of all to the vaqueros are the characteristics that have come to mark us as a people and a nation. Our passion for the great outdoors, our love of independence, and our admiration of courage and skill are all traits that, in great measure, we gained from the world's first cowboys. It is a proud inheritance. One that continues today.

SOURCES

Chapter One: Horses, Cattle, and a Special Breed of Men

The Remington quote on page 3 is from his book *Pony Tracks* (see Further Reading).

The J. Frank Dobie quote in the caption on page 5 is from his book *The Longhorns* (see Further Reading).

The quote on page 8 about longhorns is from Dobie's *The Longhorns*.

The quote about the mustang on pages 8–9 is by Marshall B. Davidson and is from his book *Life in America* (Houghton Mifflin, 1951).

Chapter Two: The Vaqueros Invent the Cowboy

The statistics concerning the number of vaqueros and the number of horses and cattle on mission ranches (page 18) is taken from Richard W. Slatta's book *Cowboys of the Americas* (see Further Reading).

The quote ending this chapter (page 23) is from David Dary's *Cowboy Culture* (see Further Reading).

Chapter Three: The Vaquero As a Person

The story of Faustina Villa (page 24) is adapted from Jane Clements Monday and Betty Bailey Colley's book *Voices from the Wild Horse Desert* (see Further Reading).

The story of Ignacio Alvarado (page 26) is also adapted from *Voices from the Wild Horse Desert*.

The Remington quotes concerning the handling of bulls (pages 26–27) are from *Pony Tracks*.

The anecdote related by an old-time cowhand concerning Mexican ranchers' honesty (page 27) is by John D. Young and is taken from the book *A Vaquero of the Brush Country* written by Young and J. Frank Dobie (see Further Reading).

The story of Eusebio García and Tom Coleman (pages 29 and 31) is adapted from J. Frank Dobie's *Cow People* (see Further Reading).

The quote about the vaquero as a man of the land (page 33) is from J. Frank Dobie's article "Ranch Americans" (*Survey Magazine*, May 1, 1931).

The quote by a former cowhand describing what a cowpuncher is (page 37) is taken from the book *The Last Cowboy* by Jane Kramer (see Further Reading).

Chapter Four: The Vaqueros' Special Skills

The Richard Henry Dana quotes on page 39 are from his book *Two Years Before the Mast* (see Further Reading).

Frederic Remington's quote concerning the vaqueros' extraordinary riding ability (pages 39–40) is from *Pony Tracks*.

J. Frank Dobie's observation about a vaquero's reliance on his rope (page 43) is taken from *A Vaquero of the Brush Country*.

The information concerning José Berrara's special roping abilities (pages 43–44) was kindly provided by the Institute of Texan Cultures.

The story of the vaquero who roped a train (page 44) is adapted from *A Vaquero of the Brush Country*.

The story of Ignatio Flores (pages 47–48) is adapted from *The Longhorns*.

The story of Tiburcio (page 48) is also adapted from *The Longhorns*.

The story of Genardo del Bosque (pages 48–49) is adapted from *The Longhorns* as well.

The story of Nestor Córdova (pages 49 and 51) is adapted from Patricia Preciado Martin's book *Images and Conversations: Mexican Americans Recall a Southwestern Past* (see Further Reading).

The expressions included in the caption on page 50 are from the book *Savvy Sayin's* by Ken Alstad (Ken Alstad Company, 1992).

Chapter Six: Tales of the Vaqueros

No one is sure just when the tall tale of Pablo Romero and Star Breast was first told, but it is very old. The version of the story presented on pages 61–64 is adapted from the writings of J. Frank Dobie, who first presented the tale in a book called *On the Open Range* and then repeated it in his *Tales of Old-Time Texas* (see Further Reading).

The two versions of the story of the headless horsemen on pages 67 and 69–70 are also adapted from *Tales of Old-Time Texas*. In his notes, J. Frank Dobie stated that he encountered the first story in *A History of Bee County* by Mrs. I. C. Madray, published in 1919. Dobie cited the story "The Headless Horseman" (published in 1924 in the journal *Frontier Times*) as the source of his account of the ranchers' revenge against the horse thief named Vidal.

The story of El Tejano (pages 72–74) is another tale that was embellished over the years. Particularly popular in Arizona, it is said to have been based upon the life of the real outlaw named William Brazelton. A spirited version of the tale is included in the book *Images and Conversations: Mexican Americans Recall a Southwestern Past*.

The caption for the picture of Joaquín Murieta (page 73) is compiled from materials found in the book *The Authentic Wild West: The Outlaws* (see Further Reading).

Chapter Seven: The Vaquero Becomes Invisible

The statistics concerning the amount of land devoted to cattle raising in the United States in the 1880s (page 76) and the effects of the winter of 1886 (page 79) are taken from the book *The American Cowboy* (see Further Reading).

The quote from President James Garfield in the caption on page 78 is from the book *American Image* by Martin W. Sandler (Contemporary Books, 1989).

The Theodore A. Dodge quote (page 81) is from his article "Some American Riders," published in the July 1891 issue of *Harper's New Monthly Magazine*.

The information about Ramón Ahumada (page 84) comes from both *Cowboys of the Americas* and the National Cowboy Hall of Fame.

Chapter Eight: Cowmen Today

The Chito Mendietta quote (page 96) about the use of helicopters in modern ranching is from *Voices from the Wild Horse Desert*.

Information concerning the Hispanic origin of the proverbs on pages 101–2 was supplied by the American Folklife Center.

The quote by Carolina Castillo Grimm in the caption on page 103 is from the introduction she wrote for *Voices from the Wild Horse Desert*.

GLOSSARY

Amansador (*amansadores*, pl.). Spanish word for a tamer of animals. Vaqueros who tamed horses were called *amansadores*.

Bandana. The large neckerchief that a vaquero wore around his neck. It was used for a variety of purposes, mainly to keep the constant dust kicked up by horses and cattle out of the wearer's eyes and mouth.

Brand, branding. The distinctive marking vaqueros burned into the hide of a calf or steer to show that the animal belonged to the ranch where the vaquero worked.

Buckaroo. The name that cowboys in various regions gave themselves; a variation of the word *vaquero.*

Californio. The name that was often given by writers and artists to vaqueros who worked on ranches in California.

Cattle drive. The term used to describe the journey over well-used trails by which cattle were taken to railroad yards hundreds of miles to the north to be then shipped by rail to slaughterhouses.

Chaparajos, chaps. The leggings that vaqueros wore for protection over their pants; from the Spanish words meaning "to cover."

Charro. A gentleman rider of Mexico; often the owner of the ranch where vaqueros worked.

Chuck wagon. The specially designed wagon that contained all the items the ranch cook used to prepare the meals the vaqueros ate while on the range or on a cattle drive.

Cincha, cinch. The leather strap that vaqueros used to secure their saddles around their horses; from the Spanish word meaning "sash" or "belt."

Compañero. The Spanish word meaning "companion."

Conquistadores. The Spaniards who came to the New World seeking to conquer the natives, make converts to Christianity, and take possession of their reported riches; from the Spanish word meaning "conqueror."

Correr el gallo. The name of a favorite vaquero contest on horseback; from the Spanish words meaning "chicken pull" or "chicken race."

Dar la vuelta. The technique introduced by the vaqueros by which they wrapped their rope around their saddle horn when roping a cow or horse; from the Spanish words meaning "turn around" or "take a turn."

Dude ranch. A modern ranch where visitors pay to take part in the activities carried out by old-time vaqueros and cowboys.

La Epcata. The process used by the vaqueros to predict the various phases of the moon; from the Spanish word *epoca* meaning "a period of time."

Figure eight. A particular type of rope toss introduced by the vaqueros.

Frijoles. The Spanish word meaning "beans."

Gaucho. A horseman or ranch worker of the plains, primarily used in Argentina and Brazil.

Lasso, lazo. The loop at the end of a vaquero's rope used to secure an animal; from the Spanish word *enlazar* meaning "to tie."

Llanero. Horsemen of the tropical plains of Venezuela and Colombia.

Longhorn. The breed of cattle first raised and tended by the vaqueros on Mexican ranches and then brought to the United States.

Luaso. A Chilean horseman.

Mangana. A particular type of rope toss used by the vaqueros; *mano* in Spanish means "hand."

Missions. The often-fortified buildings established in the New World by Catholics, where religious services were held in the Church's attempt to convert natives to Christianity.

Mustangs. The horses brought to the Americas by the Spanish; from the Spanish word *mesteño.*

Padre. The Spanish word meaning "priest" or "father."

Pan de campo. The Spanish words meaning "camp bread," which was a common food the vaqueros ate while on the range or on a cattle drive.

Paniolo. The name given to cowboys in Hawaii who originally learned their trade from the vaqueros.

Piale. A particular type of rope toss used by the vaqueros.

Reata. The Spanish word meaning "rope" made of rawhide.

Recogiendo. The Spanish word meaning "picking up," the name of a contest on horseback popular with the vaqueros.

Serape. The brightly colored cape or shawl worn by vaqueros.

Sombrero. The large broad-brimmed hat worn by vaqueros.

La sortija. A popular vaquero contest; from the Spanish term meaning the "ring race."

Tapaderas, taps. The leather stirrup coverings that vaqueros used to protect their feet while riding through rough terrain; in Spanish *tapa* means "a covering."

Tejas. The name given to the region of New Spain that became the Republic of Texas and later the state of Texas.

Tortilla. The flat bread that was a staple of the vaqueros' diet.

Trail drive. Another name for a cattle drive.

FURTHER READING

With the exception of two or three brief picture books for very young children, there have been no books about the vaqueros written for young readers. All the books listed below were written for an adult audience. Each, however, is highly readable and provides insights into the vaqueros' story.

Peggy Samuels and Harold Samuels, editors. *Collected Writings of Frederic Remington.* Garden City, New York: Doubleday, 1979.

Frederic Remington. *Pony Tracks.* Norman and London: University of Oklahoma Press, 1961.

Frederic Remington is justifiably acclaimed as one of the greatest artists and sculptors of the Old West. He was also a talented writer. These two books include Remington's vivid descriptions of vaqueros and cowboys and contain many of his drawings.

J. Frank Dobie. *Cow People.* Austin: University of Texas Press, 1964.

J. Frank Dobie. *Tales of Old-Time Texas.* Edison, New Jersey: Castle Books, 1951.

J. Frank Dobie. *The Longhorns.* Edison, New Jersey: Castle Books, 1941.

J. Frank Dobie was arguably the best and certainly the most prolific of all the writers of the old-time cowmen. Although his books are filled mainly with stories about the cowboys, one can find tales of vaqueros scattered throughout them.

Richard Henry Dana. *Two Years Before the Mast.* New York: Penguin Books, 1981.

This book is mostly about a great, true sea adventure undertaken by the author. During the initial part of his voyage Dana put into port in California where he observed vaqueros. His descriptions of the vaqueros and their activities that he encountered are fascinating to read.

Lonn Taylor and Ingrid Marr. *The American Cowboy.* New York: Harper and Row, 1983.

This book contains marvelous photographs and drawings of ranching from the earliest days to today. While the text is mostly about cowboys, it presents some valuable information about the vaqueros.

Frank Getlein. *The Lure of the Great West.* Waukesha, Wisconsin: Country Beautiful, 1973.

Paul A. Rossi and David C. Hunt. *The Art of the Old West.* New York: Alfred A. Knopf, 1971.

Among the many beautifully reproduced paintings in these two books are several depictions of vaqueros. The text accompanying these paintings is detailed and informative.

James D. Horan. *The Authentic Wild West: The Outlaws.* New York: Crown Publishers, 1976.
This book is fun to read. It's all about fabled outlaws of the Old West. It contains the best account of the fictitious Joaquín Murieta and how people came to believe that he really existed.

Richard W. Slatta. *Cowboys of the Americas.* New Haven and London: Yale University Press, 1990.
This book is the most comprehensive ever written about cattle raising in all of the Americas. It also contains many fascinating illustrations.

David Dary. *Cowboy Culture.* Lawrence: University of Kansas, 1989.
William H. Forbis. *The Cowboys.* New York: Time Life Books, 1973.
The American cowboy has been one of the most widely portrayed characters in all of literature. These two books in particular give the reader a clear understanding of the cowboy's way of life and of the debt he owed to the vaqueros.

Andy Adams. *The Log of a Cowboy: A Narrative of the Old Trail Days.* Lincoln/London: University of Nebraska Press, 1964.
John D. Young and J. Frank Dobie. *A Vaquero of the Brush Country.* Austin: University of Texas Press, 1988.
These two books contain the best firsthand accounts ever written by cowmen themselves. Andy Adams's book tells the exciting tale of an actual cattle drive. Although Young's book is titled *A Vaquero of the Brush Country,* Young was not a vaquero but a cowboy. It is another example of how the cowboys borrowed almost everything from the vaqueros, including sometimes their very name. Still, Young's book provides valuable insights into the cowmen's ways of life.

Jane Clements Monday and Betty Bailey Colley. *Voices from the Wild Horse Desert.* Austin: University of Texas Press, 1997.
This book gives an excellent account of the ways in which several generations of vaqueros and their families have contributed to the running of Texas's King and Kenedy ranches, two of the largest cattle-raising operations ever established.

Patricia Preciado Martin. *Images and Conversations: Mexican Americans Recall a Southwestern Past.* Tucson: University of Arizona Press, 1983.
In this book descendants of old-time vaqueros recall growing up in areas of Arizona dominated by Hispanic culture. The book is filled with legend and fact concerning their ancestors' ways of life.

Jane Kramer. *The Last Cowboy.* New York: Harper and Row, 1977.
Kathleen Jo Ryan. *Deep in the Heart of Texas.* Berkeley: Ten Speed Press, 1999.
Both of these books contain detailed accounts of modern ranching. Particularly interesting are the comparisons they provide between the life and world of old-time cowmen and those who tend the range today.

INDEX

(Page numbers in *italic* refer to illustrations and captions.)

Advertisements, *82*, 84–85, *87*
Africa, mustang origins in, 8
African-Americans, *20*, *20*–23, 81
Agrito, 33
Ahumada, Ramón, 84, *85*
Alvarado, Ignacio, 26
Amansadores, 49–51
Amargosa, 33
American Southwest, 10, 79
   cattle introduced into, 12
   spread of ranching to, 19–23
Argentina, 36, 37
Aztecs, 11–12

Bandanas, *25*
Bandits:
   horse thieves, 35, 67–70, *71*
   Robin Hood types, 71–75, *73*
Barbed wire, 77
Bears, *63*
   Romero's encounter with, 61–65, *65*, *66*
Becerra, Lin, 100, *101*
Beef prices, 78, 99
Bernal, Hercal, 69
Berrara, José, 43–44, 90
Big Dipper, 34
Book illustrations, *83*, 84–85, *86*
Branding, *52*, *57*
   contemporary, 93, *98*, 99

Brasil, 32
Brazil, 37
"Breaking" wild horses, 49–51, *50*
Breeding cattle, 99
Buckaroos, use of word, 23
Bueno, Juan, *58*
Bulldogging, *20*
Bull-tailing, 26–27

California, 10
   missions in, 15, *16*, *63*
Californios at the Horse Roundup, *28*
Callaghan Ranch, 29–31
Cantu, Miguel, *58*
Carbajal, Aurielio, *58*
Carbajal, V. F., *58*, 84
Catholic priests. *See* Priests
Cat's claw, 33
Cattle, *15*
   branding of, *52*, *57*, 93, *98*, 99
   breeding of, 99
   brought to New World, 10–13, *11*
   buying and selling of, 99
   dividing themselves into small groups, 35–37
   in Hawaiian Islands, 21–22
   longhorns, *5*, *5*–9, 12, *12*
   roundups of. *See* Roundups
   uses of, *16*

Cattle drives, 12, *16*, 23, 52,
    58–60
  longhorns well suited for, 8
  at night, 35
  northbound routes of, from Texas,
    19
  railroads and, 78
Cayetano, Don, 72
Chaparejos (chaps), 23, *25*
Charros, 17, 17–18
Chile, 37
Chuck wagons, 30–31, *57,*
    94–95
Cinchas (cinches), 23, *38*
Civil War, 19, 81
Claret cup, 32
Clepino, 32
Cleveland, Richard, 22
Clothing and equipment, 23, *25, 38,*
    56
Cody, William F. (Buffalo Bill),
    86–91, *88–89*
Coleman, Tom, 29–31
Colombia, 37
Columbus, Christopher, 10
Coma, 32, 33
Computers, 99
Congress of Rough Riders of the
    World, *88–89,* 91
Conquistadors, 10–11, *11,* 36
Contests, 41–43, *42*
Córdova, Nestor, 49–51, 84
Coronado, Francisco Vásquez de,
    12
Correr el gallo, 41–43, *42*
Cortés, Gregorio, 69
Cortés, Hernán, 11–12
Courage, of vaqueros, 26–27, 65
Cow Boy, 86
Cowboys, viii
  African-American, *20,* 20–23
  bull-tailing and, 27
  trained by vaqueros, 23
  turned into legends, 79–81, *82, 90,*
    91, 91–92
  vaqueros as predecessors of, 3,
    9
  white, emergence of, 20

Cowmen:
  contemporary, 93–101, *94–98,*
    100
  see also Vaqueros
"Cow sense":
  of mustangs, 8–9
  of vaqueros, 35–37
Cuernavaca, 12

Dana, Richard Henry, 39
Dar la vuelta, 45–47, *46*
Del Bosque, Genardo, 48–49
Dobie, J. Frank, *5,* 7–8, 33, 43,
    48–49
Dodge, Theodore A., 81–84

Epcata, la, 35
Equipment and clothing, 23, *25, 38,*
    56
Esquival, Antonio, 90
Expressions, derived from vaqueros,
    102

Falling, 51
Figure eight, 44–45
Flores (rancher), 67
Flores, Ignatio, 47–48

Games, 41–43, *42*
García, Eusebio, 29–31
Garfield, James, 78
Gauchos, 36
Gold, 11, 12
Golden Cities of Cíbola, 12
Gortari, Macedonio, *58*
Granjeno, 33
Grimm, Carolina Castillo,
    103
Guns, 63, 65

Harper's New Monthly Magazine,
    81–84
Harper's Weekly, 4, 59
Hawaiian Islands, 21–22
Headless horseman, 66–70
Helicopters, 95–99, *97*
Hispaniola, 10
Honesty, of vaqueros, 27–31

Horses, 35
  brought to New World, 10–13,
    11
  buying and selling of, 99
  mustangs, 6–7, 8–9, 22
  prehistoric, 10
  in roundups (*rodeos*), 5
  vaqueros' skills on, 3, 5, 39–43,
    40
  wild, herding of, *28*
  wild, taming of, 49–51, *50*
Horse thieves, 35, 67–70, 71
Huajilla, 33
Huasos, 37

Illuvia de oro, 32–33
Immigrants, 81
Indians, 66, 86

Jimenez, Melchior, *58*

Kenedy Ranch, 23, 94, 96,
    100
King Ranch, 23, 24–26, 94,
    100
Kino, Father Eusebio, 15

Lances, *15*, 41
Lazo (lasso), 43–45
*Life and Adventures of Joaquín
    Murieta, The* (Ridge), 73
Llaneros, 36
Longhorns, 5, 5–8, 12, *12*
  mustangs' "cow sense" and,
    8–9
  special value of, 7–8
  see also Cattle
Longoria, Francisco, *58*
Love, Nat, 23
Loyalty, of vaqueros, 24–26
Lucero, Eli, 84

Mangana, 45
Martínez, Rene, 96
Meals, 30–31, 35, *57*, 94–95,
    102–3
Medicinal plants, 33
Mendietta, Chito, 96–97, 101

Mexico, *12*
  cattle and horses introduced into,
    10, 11–12, 13
  charros in, *17,* 17–18
  first ranch in, 11–12
  independence of, 17
  missions in, 15–17, 18
  Spanish conquest of, 11
  Texan independence from, 19
"Mi Caballo Bayo" (my bay horse),
    68
Missions, *14–16,* 15–17, 18, *63*
Moon, *34, 35*
Moors, 8
Morning Star, 35
Mota Ranch, La, *100*
Movies, *90, 91,* 91–92
Murieta, Joaquín, *73*
Music, of vaqueros, *68,*
    68–69
Mustangs, 6–7, 8–9
  in Hawaiian Islands, 22
  see also Horses

National Cowboy Hall of Fame,
    84
Natural world, vaqueros' knowledge
    of, 31–33
Night:
  storytelling in, 61, *62,* 74
  telling time by stars in, 34–35
Nuestra Señora de los Dolores,
    15

Oil, 29–31

Padres. See Priests
Pampas, 36
Pan de campo (camp bread),
    31
Paniolos, 21, 21–22
Piale, 45
Pickett, Bill, *20*
Pickup trucks, 94–95, *96*
Pioneers, 76–78, *77, 78*
Plays, 79, *82*
Prejudice, viii, 75, 79–84
Presidios, 14

Priests (*padres*), 13
mission ranches taken away from,
   18
missions built by, *14–16, 15–17,
   63*
Proverbs, 101–2

Quirt and the Spur, The (Rye), 83

Railroads, 77–78, *78*
Ranches:
   of *charros, 17,* 17–18
   contemporary, 93–101, *94–98, 100*
   end of glory days of, 76–79
   first in New World, 11–12
   on mission property, *15, 16,*
      16–17, 18, *63*
   northward spread of, *18*
Range:
   open, closing off of, 76–77
   vaqueros' work on, *52, 53–55*
Rattlesnakes, 33
Reata, 43. *See also* Ropes and roping
Recogiendo, 41–43
Remington, Frederic, 3–5, 8, 26–27,
   39–40
Reón, Juan, 84
Retama, 32–33
Ridge, John, *73*
River crossings, *59*
Robles, Andres, *100*
Rodeos, *101*
Rodeos. See Roundups
Romero, Pablo, 61–65, *65, 66*
Ropes and roping:
   of bears, 63–65, *65*
   construction of, *44*
   in different lengths, *45*
   vaqueros' skills in, 3, *20,* 43–47,
      44–46
Roundups (*rodeos*), 3–5, 23, 52, *56,
   57*
   contemporary, 93–99, *97*
   of wild horses, *28*
Rye, Edgar, *83*

Saddles, 23
Sanchez, Anastacio, *58*

Serapes, 5, 56
Serra, Father Junípero, 15
Shower of gold, 32–33
Silva, Rogerio, 100, 101
Snake bites, 33
Sombreros, *25*
Sortija, la, 41
Southwest. *See* American Southwest
Spain, 41
   conquistadors from, 10–11, *11,*
      36
   horses and cattle sent to New
      World from, 10, *11*
   horses brought from Africa to, 8
   Mexican liberation from, 17
Spanish dagger, 33
Spurs, *38*
Stagecoach robberies, 72–75,
   86
Stahl, Jessie, 23
Stampedes, 26, *60*
Star Breast, 62–65, *65*
Stars, 34–35
Stirrups, *38*
Storytelling, 61–75, *62, 74*
   bandits and, 71–73, *73*
   headless horseman and, 66–70
   heroic vaquero deeds and,
      61–65
Strays, 26, 37, 95–96
Supernatural, vaqueros' belief in, 65,
   67, *71,* 74, 75

Tapaderas (taps), 23, *38*
Taylor, Creed, 67–70
Tejano, El (The Texan), 71–75
Texas, 10, 79
   independence of, 19
   northbound routes of cattle drives
      from, *19*
   spread of ranching to, 19–23
Thorns, *32,* 32–33, *38*
Tiburcio (vaquero), 48
Time, stars and, 34–35
"Toro Moro, El," 68
Tracking skills, 47–49

Uruguay, 37

Vancouver, George, 21
Vaqueros, *4, 12, 13, 15*
  clothing and equipment of, 23, *25, 38, 56*
  contemporary, 93–101, *94–98, 100*
  courage of, 26–27, *65*
  cowboys trained by, 23
  "cow sense" of, 35–37
  determined to tame any beast, *29*
  diet of, 30–31, 102–3
  distorted and negative depictions of, 81–84, *83,* 91
  games and contests of, 41–43, *42*
  Hawaiian, *21,* 21–22
  honesty of, 27–31
  horsemanship of, 3, *5,* 39–43, *40*
  knowledge of, 31–33
  loyalty of, 24–26
  on mission ranches, *15, 16,* 16–17, 18, *63*
  music of, *68,* 68–69
  origin of word, 3
  popular culture influenced by, 101–3
  prejudice against, viii, *75,* 79–84
  rope skills of, 3, *20,* 43–47, *44–46*
  stars as timepieces for, 34–35
  storytelling of, 61–75, *62, 74*
  tracking skills of, 47–49
  training of, 39, 43
  wild horses tamed by, 49–51, *50*
  in Wild West Shows, 43, 85–91, *88–89*
  working day of, 52, *53–60*
  working for *charros,* 18
Vegetation, 31–33, *32*
Venezuela, 36, 37
Veracruz, Mexico, *12*
Vidal (horse thief), 67–70
Viejo Ranch, 48
Villa, Faustina, 24, 84
Villalobos, Gregorio de, 11
Virginian, The (Wister), *80*

Walking, vaqueros' gait and, 39
Wallace, Bigfoot, 67–70
Weather, *34,* 79
Westerns, *90, 91,* 91–92
Wild West Shows, 43, 85–91, *88–89*
Winter of 1886, 79
Wister, Owen, *80*

Zorro, 91

GAYLORD R